"Read, heed, and lead your visibility with this dangerously-powerful wisdom! At last, a treasure I trust 100% in the too-often dog-eat-dog world that is publicity."

>Andrea J. Lee, Author of *We Need to Talk and Multiple Streams of Coaching Income*

"Media interviews are pivotal in getting your best work to the people who need it. In this wonderful book, Joanne demystifies what it takes to land and nail them—from winning the inner to making a plan to preparing for the interview so you shine. Get this book, practice its insights, and become the media darling hosts are looking to showcase."

>Charlie Gilkey, Author of *Start Finishing* and Founder/CEO of Productive Flourishing and Momentum

"In this era of instant fame and viral publicity, we all need an experienced sherpa to get us through it. Those mistakes you make? The Internet will not forget them, and they can cost you big time. Joanne McCall is the seasoned guide we all need. Her decades of PR and media polishing, including her stints as a radio and podcast host and producer, have baked in her authority in the field. This book is loaded with her wisdom. I'll be referring back to it for years to come. Excellent advice!"

>Suzanne Falter, Author of *The Extremely Busy Woman's Guide to Self-Care*

"As a long-time radio host, I am always delighted when one of Joanne McCall's clients is booked because I know we will have a great show. Steeped in the insights and wisdom that Joanne shares in *Media Darling: Shine Through Every Interview*, they are reliably outstanding guests, mentored by Joanne to express themselves confidently, clearly, and interestingly."

> John Erickson, News Director and Morning Show Co-Host on *iHeart Media*

"Joanne McCall is one of the most gifted and experienced media publicists you will ever encounter. She captures and shares the best of her eye-opening stories and insights from years of helping people achieve success with media. This is a must-read book for anyone striving to get reviews, feature stories, or conduct interviews with reporters, journalists, or editors with prime media or online influencers."

> Paul J. Krupin, Creator and Founder of Direct Contact PR and Presari

Media Darling

Shine Through Every Interview

Joanne McCall

THE WRIGHT
PUBLISHING
HOUSE

Portland, Oregon

Media Darling: Shine Through Every Interview

Copyright 2022 by Joanne McCall

All rights reserved. Printed in the United States of America.
No part of this publication may be reproduced, distributed, or transmitted in any form or by any means, including photocopying, recording, or other electronic or mechanical methods, without the prior written permission from the authors, except in the case of brief quotations embodied in critical reviews and certain other non-commercial uses permitted by copyright law.

The Wright Publishing House
8200 SW 184 Ave
Beaverton, OR 97007
www.joannemccall.com
JoanneMcCall.com/books

ISBN: 978-1-7360950-0-3 soft cover
ISBN: 978-1-7360950-1-0 hard cover
ISBN: 978-1-7360950-2-7 eBook

Cover design by Pankaj Singh Renu

Why Read This Book

You know you have a great message to share with the world. You want to be more visible and help others by sharing your expertise. You want to and should be doing media interviews, but how? Trying to navigate the media landscape can be intimidating, even when you are an experienced, competent professional. And let's face it, you want to look and sound good doing it. There are plenty of people who tell you to "just flip on the camera and wing it!" But not so fast. After years of media training, branding, book publicity, and marketing, Joanne McCall shares the good news that there has never been a better time than right now for learning how to present yourself and your book effectively through the many media channels available. These highly coveted earned-media opportunities give you substantial credibility and exposure to huge audiences. Additionally, there are significant opportunities through your own media channels and those of your partners and affiliates. But you must shine.

A Media Darling knows what is trending in media.

Mom was right when she said you never get a second chance to give a great first impression, but the second-best time to do it is right now. This book is a step-by-step guide to becoming a Media Darling and contains the tools needed to succeed. This is about coming across as the amazing influencer you know you are (or could be) and doing it in such a way that those watching you know you are too.

Written by a Leading Expert in Media, Marketing, and Book Publicity

Publicist, media insider, trainer, and coach Joanne McCall helps influencers, nonfiction authors, and business leaders become Media Darlings, as the media calls them. As a licensed Business Master Practitioner of Neuro-Linguistic Programming (NLP) and a licensed Advanced Hypnotic Practitioner, her secret sauce is not only positioning, securing, and helping authors and influencers capture media attention and deliver compelling interviews but also helping them enjoy the process while creating and developing their own media empire. On a first-name basis with hundreds of top-rung producers, editors, writers, and journalists, Joanne secures coverage for clients including Brian Tracy, Ken Blanchard, Dave Ramsey, Geneen Roth, Dr. Donna Stoneham, The Deepak Chopra Center for Wellbeing, the co-founder of NLP, Dr. Richard Bandler, and many others. Her highly acclaimed media strategy sessions help authors become Media Darlings, and her Media Darling finishing school gets them visible. JoanneMcCall.com/books

To bring Joanne McCall to your organization or conference as a speaker or to consult with her one-on-one on how you can become a Media Darling, contact her at **JoanneMcCall.com** or (503) 642-4191.

Table of Contents

Why Read This Book v
Written by a leading expert in media, marketing, and book publicity vii
Essential Media Terminology 1
Chapter 1: What is a Media Darling? 5
Chapter 2: The Inner and Outer Games of Media 19
Chapter 3: Getting Noticed in an Incredibly Noisy World 31
Chapter 4: What Do I Talk About? 45
Chapter 5: What Kind of Interview Are You Doing? 59
Chapter 6: On-Camera Tips 77
Chapter 7: The Interview Itself 89
Chapter 8: Surprise! That Did Not Just Happen! 105
Chapter 9: Top Media No-Nos 119
Chapter 10: Top Media Yeses 131
Chapter 11: Common Questions Asked by Authors and Brand Influencers 143
Chapter 12: Now What? How To Take These Skills and Apply Them to Your Media Outreach 161
Chapter 13: Additional Resources 173
A Sneak Peek: Joanne McCall's Next Book! 175
Author's Final Thoughts 179
P.S. 184
You Are Invited! 185

Essential Media Terminology

Below is a list of terms or jargon commonly used in media. They will be helpful for you to know when landing interviews:

Beat – A beat is an area covered by the journalist, producer, or outlet, such as business, politics, education, health, or entertainment. There are subcategories within each. For example, business includes the workplace, careers, leadership and management, and human resources, among others.

Key messages – These are the fundamental points within your book that you want to share during your interviews.

Sound bite – Sound bites can be talking points, stories, vignettes, facts, stats, or anecdotes. They are often shocking and provocative, moving, and memorable. They are essential messages, and they need to be a natural part of the conversation. An interview consisting only of sound bites would be annoying, so think of them as the sizzle on the steak—like a spice used in cooking. A little dash of this and a little dash of something else creates the magic and makes it memorable and very sticky.

Media Darling

Talking points – When a producer asks you to send your talking points, they are asking for a list of bullet points, discussion points, or topics that you will address during your interview. These may be different from your list of key messages from your book. An interview that covers, say, one topic in your book would only have key messages related to that—not all the messages in the book. Make sure you have a list of what you sent to the producer, so you stay on target.

Technical Terms

A-roll – A-roll is the footage shot by the primary camera where there are multiple cameras available.

B-roll – This background footage runs underneath a voice-over that a news reporter or an interview host is doing. Sometimes news crews will shoot B-roll, and sometimes the producer will ask you or your publicist to supply B-roll. Talking heads do not make for a great show when you are doing an on-camera interview, so B-roll fills a purpose. The time to think about it and get it produced is now before you land an interview—unless you like that kind of pressure. Back in the days of *The Oprah Winfrey Show*, producers were fond of introducing guests by first showing B-roll. If you look at any old footage, which is easy to do on YouTube, you will see how they put it together.

Boom – This microphone is at the end of a boom pole and captures the sound near the action. I use this type of mic in my home studio with the boom pole attached to the side of the desk. You cannot beat the high-quality sound that boom mics produce, which is necessary for some top-tier, high-quality shows.

Essential Media Terminology

Chyron (pronounced ˈkīrän) – This refers to the graphics or words at the bottom of a screen. Often when you are doing an interview, your name and the title of your book will appear there for at least part of the interview.

Crawl – This is when text "crawls" along the bottom of a screen during an interview or news segment. Sometimes it pertains to the current interview, but often it is unrelated to what is on the screen and features other news flashes. News networks and cable outlets are fond of these.

Green screen – The best green screen backdrop can eliminate unsightly objects and scenery, whether streaming from a home office or conducting a photoshoot in a studio. A green screen can also be used to superimpose special effects and scenery during editing. Green screens are common in home offices now, but be sure you get a high-quality one that doesn't create a "halo" around the outline of the head.

Hot mic – A hot mic is a microphone that is turned on and is "live."

Lapel or lavalier mic – When in studio for an interview, a lapel mic or lavalier mic will be clipped onto your clothing. The mic pack—a small box housing the transmitter and battery pack—will also be clipped to your clothing somewhere it will not be seen, such as the back of your belt or even inside a dress or shirt. Consider this when choosing your clothing for an interview. For women, a dress is not advisable. It is embarrassing when the sound guy or gal has to position that mic correctly.

Media Darling

Mic pack – This electronic pack transfers the signal from a lapel mic to the camera or soundboard.

Morning and afternoon drive times – This refers to the hours when most commuters are in the car on their way to or from work. It applies to radio, both terrestrial and satellite radio.

Remote interview or live shot – Common during the days of the pandemic, a remote interview is when the interviewer is in a different location than the interviewee. They can be conducted via Skype, Zoom, or other video conferencing software applications and systems. You may be asked to go to a studio to shoot a remote interview with an interviewer located elsewhere. I had a client in a studio in Los Angeles for an interview with Wolf Blitzer on *CNN* in New York, so there are different possibilities for remote interviews.

Stills – Stills are simply photographs, as in *still images* instead of *moving images*. Print media outlets will often ask for still photographs that can support the story being written, although now it is even more common to be asked to supply a slide show for them, which is a series of still shots. Everyone is multi-media now, so producers might also ask for stills to be used in producing their stories which can then be added to their websites in print, video, or audio files.

Chapter 1
What is a Media Darling?

A train wreck was unfolding before my eyes. I should have turned away, but I couldn't. I had to know what was going to happen next.

This train wreck was on Instagram. As I was scrolling through my feed, I discovered that one of my connections was hosting a live interview, and I was curious about what she was saying. Pausing on her video image, up came the volume with her clearly agitated voice complaining, "I wonder where she can be? We arranged a time to do this interview, and it is right now. She should have been here two minutes ago. She's late! How can she be late like this? I can't believe it!"

A Media Darling is never late.

I wondered who had the audacity to be late to this important interview. Then my publicist brain took over and thought, "Why is this interviewer calling out her guest like this? Doesn't she realize her guest is going to see this later and will likely be offended by it?"

Finally, up popped the guest, and everyone was all smiles. The guest was oblivious to what had just unfolded about her only moments before. She'd know soon enough.

That has to be in my book, I thought. *It is a perfect and obvious example of what a Media Darling is not.*

Being a Media Darling usually refers to the guest or the interviewee, but now that we are ALL the media, it applies to both roles: guest and host.

We are all the media.

Most people who have a business, brand, and book are not only seeking interviews on other platforms but are also conducting them as they build out their own platforms or media empires. This is often in the form of videos, podcasts, blogs, or social media live shots. Although we are all the media, this book will focus on you as the guest doing interviews. Another book is coming specifically for hosts.

What is a Media Darling?

Back to the train wreck. Some might call the host's reaction to her guest being late as "being authentic," but it is rude. It showed someone not very experienced at doing interviews. The idea is usually to make your guest feel welcome, not call them out before an interview and then turn all nicey-nicey when they arrive.

As the guest of a show, you can help the host by sending them some material beforehand that they can resort to if they need to fill time. You do not want to say, "I am going to be late, so use this to fill." Never plan to be late, but you can offer some background material that they can share, which can set up the interview very nicely.

The good and the bad news about working with media people is that surprises happen. There were so many surprises in my earlier radio career that prepared me for just about anything. While those experiences weren't exactly enjoyable, they shaped me as a professional. I learned a lot, and you will too.

A Media Darling is nimble.

With the stories and suggestions in this book, you can learn from my experience. Surprises show us where we are in our development, teach us, and allow us to get better.

Media Darling

I was recently invited to speak on the topic of book publicity in a virtual Clubhouse room. About an hour into the session, the host was suddenly dropped from the room. Who knows why? Something buggy with the app, and I was suddenly thrown into the moderator role. Surprise!

I knew the host would try to get back in, so I acknowledged what happened, that she would be back, and picked up the conversation where she left off. It was a surprise, but the transition was smooth, and all was well until she could get back into the room.

Before you learn to deal with them, unexpected surprises can be clunky and awkward. But once you get used to dealing with surprises, it can be fun to see how elegant and capable you have become. That feels good.

In addition to social media, there are more traditional media outlets such as television, radio, print, and online channels. Live video interviews, podcasts, radio, and interviews with journalists all require preparation.

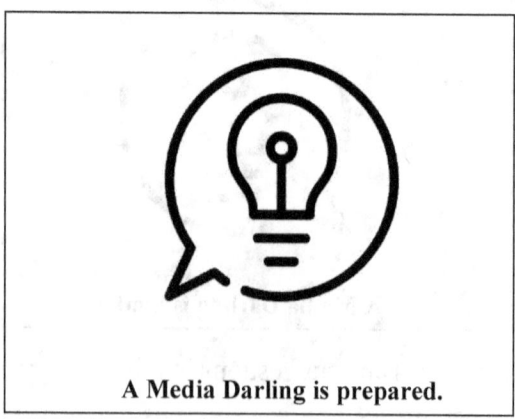

A Media Darling is prepared.

What is a Media Darling?

We will cover the fundamentals that will generalize throughout the various media platforms, which will help you across all of them. It will apply to what is coming down the pike technology-wise, and we will look at specific tips for various platforms.

Dealing with unexpected events is not the only skill to develop. Sometimes to be a Media Darling, you have to break some bad habits. Have you ever felt "media envy" or "visibility envy?"

Have your ever felt "media envy?"

You know what I mean. You get that gnawing, uncomfortable feeling when you see someone else doing an interview, a video, a post, an appearance on an influential podcast, or some other significant media opportunity that you think you should be doing.

It could be someone who does similar work to you, but not necessarily. You may secretly think you are much better than they are, or maybe you worry that you are not. It is even worse when it is someone you know within your niche. Maybe they even started in their profession after you did. Perhaps they are ten years younger, and you have so much more experience to share.

Media Darling

"Media envy" can feel like a punch in the stomach or like a shot of adrenaline racing through your veins. For most people, it is not a desirable feeling, so you may find yourself going into total denial, thinking, *That did not just happen.* You may decide you need a good distraction and find yourself turning to social media to see what everyone else is up to or clicking to watch some of those very addicting *First Time Hearing* videos on YouTube, or maybe even Netflix binge-watching while diving into that Ben & Jerry's pint in the freezer. Those who are more health-oriented may go for a good, long run or bike ride to take the edge off those feelings (definitely the healthiest option).

Worst of all, you have to admit they are doing a fantastic job. Ugh! Then, to add insult to injury, they are getting all kinds of likes, kudos, and expressions of how great they are doing, and probably plenty of money and more business opportunities. You might feel like you are being left behind. The endless reasons for media envy are unimportant, but clearly, they need to be addressed.

The mind can be stubborn, and it sometimes has trouble letting things go. No matter what you do to get relief, the thought sneaks back in: *Maybe I am not tech-savvy enough. Maybe I can't keep up.* After all, they are the ones putting themselves out there and getting the attention, not you. Maybe you know you can do this, but the question is how? And that is what we are going to delve into within these pages. The mind can be a tyrant when left to its own devices, so let's get you headed in the right direction and feeling good about it.

As my good friend, Andrea J. Lee, who also happens to

be an outstanding business coach, once told me, in those moments when you experience that rush of feeling media or visibility envy, "Take it like a vitamin pill."

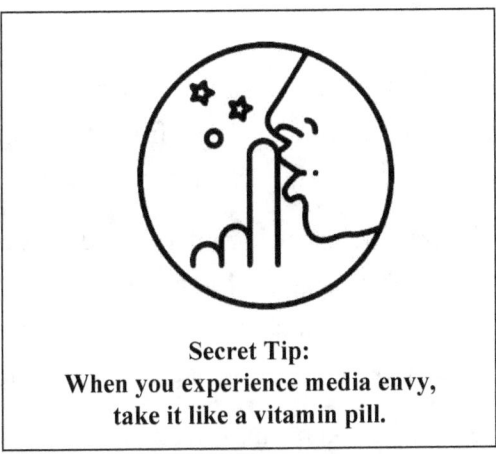

Secret Tip:
When you experience media envy, take it like a vitamin pill.

"Make that energy work for you and go on to do something even better." Great advice. I am passing the suggestion along. Then it is time to reflect before taking action.

WHAT IS A MEDIA DARLING?

There are fundamentals to being a Media Darling that apply to every situation.

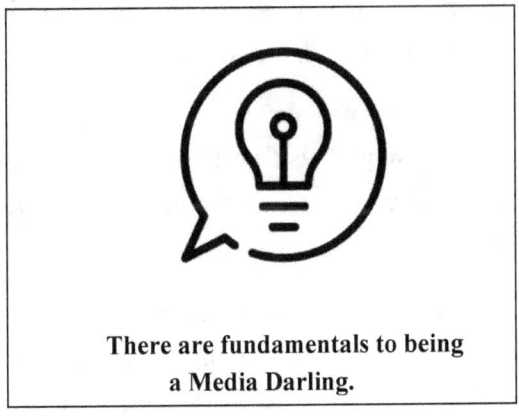

There are fundamentals to being a Media Darling.

Media Darling

They are called fundamentals for a reason. Learn them. Know them. Absorb them. Practice them.

Here is an acronym that spells out the ideal attitude of a Media Darling:

M – Motivated. A Media Darling is motivated to share the message with those who will benefit from it and, therefore, is inspired to do what it takes to land the interviews.

E – Energized. When being interviewed, most people do not express enough energy. A Media Darling is enthusiastic about their message, and it comes across. Otherwise, how can you expect others to feel that way and embrace your message?

D – Directed. They know the direction of an interview, how to bring it back when it goes off track, and how to tee up the next question so as not to make the host do all the work.

I – Interesting. Do not be boring.

A – Attitude. It is everything. Now and then, things will go wrong (see the chapter on surprises). How you deal with surprises determines how others see you.

D – Determined. It is work to pitch and land interviews. Then you must deliver well, too. It takes determination to keep going.

A – Amiable. Who doesn't prefer friendly people? There are enough grouches and prima donnas in the world. Do not be one of them.

R – Relatable. If the audience hearing your message cannot relate to what you are saying, you might as well stop doing interviews. A Media Darling is relatable.

What is a Media Darling?

L – Lightness. Even when covering a serious subject, do not take yourself too seriously.

I – Illuminating. The job of a Media Darling is to enlighten the audience.

N – Nimble. A Media Darling is flexible and able to pivot no matter what comes up in an interview.

G – Giving. A Media Darling is generous and does not hold back useful information. They share as much as they can in the time allotted. Do this, and the audience will think, That person shared so much here. Imagine how much is in their book!"

For a quick cheat sheet on this and other valuable resources, please visit **JoanneMcCall.com/books**.

It is time to embrace becoming a Media Darling. A big part of that is taking every appropriate opportunity that comes your way and shaping it in the direction you want to go. We were not born knowing how to deliver great interviews, how to deal with impostor syndrome, or how to let our charisma shine. We were not born with an understanding of media etiquette, pitching media, or how to stay cool in the face of surprises. These are skills that one can develop, and doing so will help you be successful now and throughout your future.

A Media Darling is someone who:

- ✓ makes it all seem effortless;
- ✓ is easy to work with, so they get invited for return appearances;
- ✓ creates great content for their own media channels;

- ✓ knows how to be exceptional on other platforms;
- ✓ makes the host look good;
- ✓ thinks like an editor or producer and knows the culture of the show or publication before pitching them;
- ✓ appropriately presents themself, is genuine and authentic, and is at their very best;
- ✓ understands various platforms and how to work with them;
- ✓ is a great guest and delivers a great interview;
- ✓ finds, reaches out to, and appropriately pitches media;
- ✓ is unique in their approach; and
- ✓ can poke fun at themself in an endearing way.

Interviews stick around in this age of digital media, so you want to put forth your best.

A Media Darling is not:

- ✗ **A prima donna.** This is challenging for some because within their area of influence, they are used to others deferring to them. However, they may be completely unknown in the media. Success in one area does not automatically transfer over to another. Prima donnas have a tough time understanding this.

- ✗ **Late to interviews.** Ever. It might be forgivable if your plane was diverted, you were stuck in a hurricane, or there was blood involved. Of course, there are times when life gets in the way, but being busy is not an appropriate reason for missing a scheduled interview.

What is a Media Darling?

- **Unresponsive or slow to respond.** Top-tier media will move on to the next expert in line if they have trouble reaching you. After six months of trying, *The Wall Street Journal* finally gave the green light to an interview with my client but gave me only five minutes to get him on the phone with the columnist before they would move on to the next person.

- **Focused only on themselves.** The job of a Media Darling is to make the producer look good, the host look good, and the show look good. Then the Media Darling will be perceived as someone they will want to interview again.

- **A complainer.** Life is challenging enough without having someone complain when things go awry. Media Darlings look for solutions and keep a positive attitude.

- **Someone who caves under pressure or surprises.** This is why media training is so important. Anticipate any tough questions and work with a media coach to produce the best response.

- **Annoyed when the host has not read their book.** Most of them do not. It is one reason creating a press kit is important.

- **Someone who says, "I am beyond this kind of interview."** Not every interview is going to be top-tier. You often have to fill in the lower tiers even to get a shot at the big media brands. No one has to take a chance on a guest anymore.

No one has to take a chance on a guest anymore.

They will want to see you in action before they even consider having you on, so do not say no to the smaller opportunities. You need that coverage too. However, it needs to be an interview that makes sense for you to do, meaning the outlet actually covers your topic. Occasionally you may get a request that seems very unusual. Clarify the request before you turn it down.

"Top-tier" refers to the most prominent media brands with the biggest audiences, such as *The New York Times*, *CNN*, *Fox News*, *The Washington Post*, *The Wall Street Journal*, to name just a few. They are certainly worth putting on your dream list for coverage, but no one starts at the top. It takes work to be covered by a top-tier media outlet. In my company, McCall Media Group, we have had the good fortune of working with many of the best authors and experts, including Brian Tracy, Ken Blanchard, Dr. Richard Bandler, Geneen Roth, Dave Ramsey, Andy Andrews, and many others. We have also enjoyed working with authors, speakers, consultants, coaches, trainers, entrepreneurs, and influencers who do not have the same national recognition, but that was not their vision or

What is a Media Darling?

objective. They wanted to be well known within their niche and secure a greater following and more business, and that is what we did by helping them become Media Darlings.

Whether you are looking to be an influencer, a national figure, a local one in your geographic region, or a big fish in your particular niche, media appearances expose you to more people and help you grow your audience and build your list. It also gives you immense credibility. You can use the media logos on your website and share links with your networks. Doing earned media interviews ensures your coverage will stay around, unlike being at the mercy of algorithms that change, and then so does your appearance. It may disappear forever.

Earned Media is the exposure you get by jumping through some hoops to get the interview or coverage.

This book is not about what equipment to buy or what lighting to purchase to look your best. There are plenty of places where you can find that simply by searching the internet.

The information we cover here is not readily available elsewhere. It results from my work with media and many different clients and books. It is what I have found that works and what does not.

You and your book are unique. Therefore, your ideas and outreach will be unique. The tips, ideas, and strategies within this book will help you develop what will work best for you.

If you embrace the ideas here and take them to heart, you will become the Media Darling you know you are meant to be. Let's get started.

Chapter 2
The Inner and Outer Games of Media

There are two sides to every situation: heads and tails, yes and no, yin and yang, pros and cons, right and wrong, up and down, inner and outer. The last one is our focus—the inner and the outer games of media. Most people focus on the outer game, not even aware of the inner game. However, when you learn about the inner game and put your attention there first, you can tap into your inner resources, your superpower, and that is where the real magic happens. We will first peek at the outer game and work our way back to the inner to show how true this is.

The Outer Game

We are all the media now. You only have to look around to see how much media content we share—people with their eyes fixated on their smartphones, hyper-connected with social media, recording video as they shop in a store with intentions of loading it onto their YouTube channel, or pulling out their cameras as they witness an event happening near them that they think others should see. Because we see it happening all around us, it is easy to get into comparisons with people and think, *Hey, I could do that. Let me just flip on a video recorder and wing it.* This is rarely a good idea. Of course, there are exceptions for filming important "real-time" events, but having some media training first will help you.

Perhaps we see the home page or cover of *The New York Times* or some other highly trafficked website and think, *It looks so easy to be there. Why aren't I there yet? This is taking too long.*

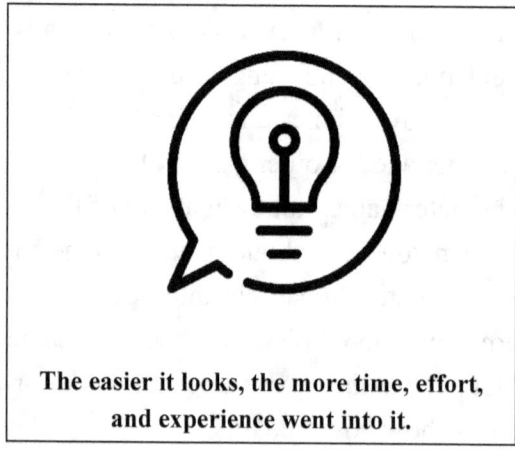

The easier it looks, the more time, effort, and experience went into it.

Even though it all looks effortless, it still takes a lot of skill, talent, and numbers to get the top-tier media to cover you. An exception is if you commit some heinous crime. Then, we could get you everywhere in minutes, but obviously, that is not a great way to do it. Aside from that, it takes effort, persistence, and a thick skin. Some say you have to fight for it if you really want it, and you can accomplish a great deal of "fighting," but there is another way.

The Inner and Outer Games of Media

Having worked with thousands of clients, I can confidently tell you the one thing that helps an author, thought leader, or business leader more than anything else. Those who use this are always more successful than those who do not, and the best part is that it does not require a lot of inner turmoil and fighting with yourself to *set those goals and just do it!* Only you and you alone can do this to improve your visibility and secure top-tier media. It is what I call the Inner Game of Media.

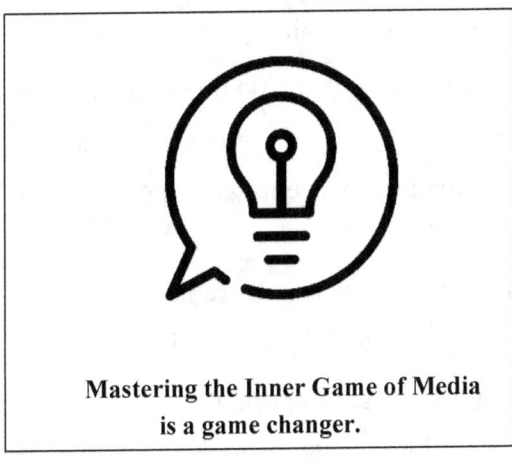

Mastering the Inner Game of Media is a game changer.

Do not get me wrong. You still have to be an expert in your field. You still have to have the credentials needed to be seen and regarded as an expert, you still have to write a great book, you still need a platform, and you have to be visible.

The outer game consists of many components, including:

- developing a brand and infusing your key messages,
- designing your overall book campaign,
- identifying and zooming in on appropriate media,
- crafting the perfect pitch for each media outlet,
- creating and pulling together the media contacts you

want to target,
- figuring out which channels to pitch and how to reach the appropriate people,
- doing the actual pitching,
- follow up, follow up, follow up,
- booking and delivering great interviews,
- tapping into appropriate ways to use the coverage to increase your visibility,
- designing various marketing campaigns that sell the book,
- participating in events and speaking opportunities, and
- ad infinitum because there is always more publicity and marketing that can be done.

All of the above are important. Critical, even. However, mastering the Inner Game of Media™ is what will get you there and make it fun along the way.

WHY IS THE INNER GAME NEGLECTED?

It is very easy to neglect something when you do not even know it exists. We get so focused on what is going on "out there" that people often forget that what takes place in their minds is the most important component.

Some people do not believe in an inner game.

A lot of people fit into this camp. It does not occur to them that a certain mindset can help them attain their vision and with less effort. These type-A people are all about doing, driving forward, taking action, making things happen, and rarely stopping. These individuals are totally into motivation and believe if they just work hard enough and long enough, they will make it happen.

This strategy works to a certain extent, and many have gone far with this attitude, but the results rarely match what the author envisioned, and it was all done with a lot of angst and effort and not a lot of fun along the way. If you are constantly pushing against yourself, you end up spinning your wheels, wasting energy that could be spent making more things happen. Again, you get things done but at the cost of your peace of mind and well-being.

Some believe the inner game is only about creating goals and mapping out how to attain them.

Every year around New Year's Day, I write an article or a blog post on why goals do not work. It is called "My Ungoals List," and every year, there is massive pushback from a lot of people when it appears on various social media sites. The blog post receives feedback like, "You must not be able to get anything done if you do not know enough to set goals," or "If you do not set goals, you do not know where you are going, and you certainly can't get to where you want to go if you do not say where it is." These are all laughable if you look at all that can be accomplished in a day.

They mean well. But you do not know what you do not know, and when you master the inner game, there is little to no resistance inside you to push against. All your energy is moving in the same direction toward what you want. When you do not have any resistance coursing through your body, causing you to either fight and struggle with it or wildly procrastinate, you can accomplish a tremendous amount without feeling tired and dragged down. You are effectively pulled toward your desires, not fighting with yourself to do what needs to be done. You are pulled toward them because you know it is what you are meant to do, you want to do it, and most importantly, it feels good. Imagine how much further you can get when you feel pulled toward your destiny rather than fighting and demanding it.

One thing I discovered through publicly posting the ungoals piece was that many people reacted to the headline without reading the article. Many of the responses would have been different if they had read it because not setting SMART goals (an acronym meaning: strategic, measurable, achievable, relevant, and timely) does not mean not having a direction and a plan. (Side note: If you are going to comment on someone's article or post, read it first.)

If you are going to comment on someone's article or post, read it first.

Thankfully, there were many positive responses to the piece, too, so many people read it and understood what it expressed.

In addition, rather than being dismayed, disappointed, or hurt by the negative comments, this feedback was gold. It became clear that you can get buckets of visibility and attention with just a headline, which is another reason not to sweat so much about what you write. Your headline shouldn't be some quick afterthought or a quick couple of search words. You want to think about what you are trying to motivate people to do or react to and then craft the perfect headline.

More on the Inner Game

The Inner Game of Media is much more than setting goals, figuring out your direction, and making plans. It happens before any of that. It is what happens within your mind. It is what you say to yourself every day or as you are beginning a creative endeavor. It is the feeling you generate internally about what you are doing. If you talk to yourself in the right way, feeling positive and enthusiastic about what you are undertaking, you will get started on the right foot. But most people give this little thought or are unconscious about what they say to themselves and then wonder why they have to push against themselves to get what they want. Sometimes they reach their goal, sometimes they do not, but it is always with much angst.

For example, let's say you made a New Year's resolution to lose ten pounds. You did the SMART goal ritual, and now you are motivated to go to the gym. So far, so good, but then come the cravings for chocolate cake, potato chips, or a beer or glass of wine, whatever your temptation is; instead of simply dismissing that thought and replacing it with something else, the inner fight begins. You start repeating to yourself, *I am not going to eat that cake. I am not going to eat that cake!* and the next thing you know, you are in the kitchen cutting a huge piece of cake. And the worst part is, you are not even enjoying it, but rather as soon as you have finished it, you start to tell yourself how weak you are and question what is wrong with you. Aren't you sick of that pattern yet? Let's finally put that to rest.

People do this when promoting their books too. They do it when securing interviews. They do it when taking steps to put themselves out there and become visible. They do it when they are not sure what steps to take next. Procrastination, fear, frustration, and hesitation get in the way and make them think that they are weak. Or sometimes they deny they feel that way and push even harder. They get up early, reach out to media trying to set up interviews, and wonder why no one is getting back to them. They have not taken care of their state yet.

Extremely Simple Recipe

Procrastination or fear makes everything more difficult. Or even impossible. There is nothing worse than fighting with yourself because it is often unconscious. You do not know you are fighting with yourself; you just know you feel bad. At least when you are fighting with others, there is a winner and a loser. I am not saying this is great for relationships, but at least there will be an end to the struggle. When you fight yourself, it can go on for years, and you just get worn down, do not get much done, and you end up feeling terrible or admitting you are a failure. This is beyond sad.

Chances are it has been going on for a long time, so long that it just seems to be a part of us, but it is not. It is a bad habit, and bad habits can be changed, not through goal setting, which sets up the struggle and the inner battle in the first place, but through other techniques and tools that can change this automatic behavior.

If you want to be very successful with your book, get top-tier media interviews, and be asked to speak at prestigious organizations, but some little voice in the back of your head whispers, *Who are you kidding?*—that needs addressing. Of course, you must first become conscious that it is there.

Sometimes that unconscious voice causes one to have trouble defining what they want. When asked what they want, whether by someone else or themselves, they just do not know. Or they have an idea but can't commit to it because *What if it is not perfect? What if I change my mind? How will I make this happen? It is going to cost too much money. I do not have time. I am overwhelmed.*

Do you think anyone can make good decisions when they are thinking like that?

The Inner Game of Media makes all the difference. There are numerous "problems" that can be eliminated simply by playing the game well, including removing resistance, procrastination, overwhelm, and the sense of *Who do I think I am to think I can do this?* Not getting the results you say you want is a clue that something else is going on in the subconscious.

If you are not getting the results you say you want, that is a clue that something else is going on.

There are two forces inside us when deciding what we want. One is resistance, and the other is desire. There is magic when you set directions or *ungoals,* and then create internal feelings that pull you automatically toward what you want rather than creating some kind of internal fight.

I had a client who is a good example of this. Let's call her Susan. Susan had huge dreams, but something always got in the way when making them happen. She checked with people in her online community and took their advice, although none of them were media professionals. She was late for interviews and missed other important deadlines. But rather than notice what she was doing, she blamed other people and other circumstances for her problems.

Sometimes things operate outside of our conscious awareness. Pay attention to the results you are getting. That will not only tell you what is working and what is not working, but it will also give you important feedback that something is going on with your Inner Game.

Some people have trouble getting started. They say they are going to start doing Instagram or Facebook Lives, but then never do them. They say they are going to reach out to the media but never seem to know how to make that happen. They often purchase multiple online programs or hire an expensive business and accountability coach, thinking that will jumpstart them. I am sure they learn some good information, but learning it is not enough. You have to make it your own by putting it into action.

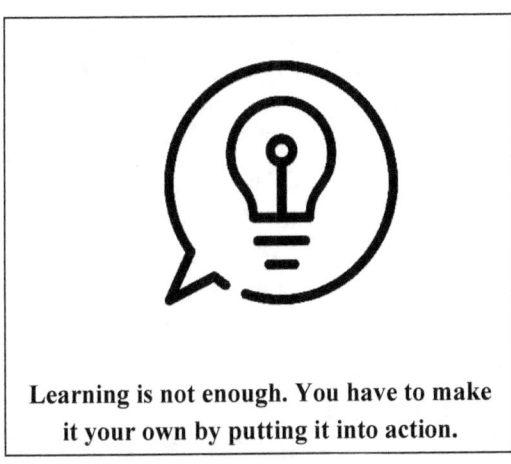

Learning is not enough. You have to make it your own by putting it into action.

Until then, it is just theory. Be careful if you find yourself going from program to program. This is another indication of internal struggle.

This inner game begins long before the outer game, and then they flow together. Plenty of people say they want visibility and exposure and then have trouble making it happen.

I had a client who wrote an amazing book that many people loved. The media responded to the campaigns we put together, but then he would miss interviews, could not get something written, or did not have time on his schedule to respond to media requests. His internal messages got in the way. That was frustrating for everyone involved.

If you are not getting what you say you want or have trouble even starting, it could mean you have old, internal messages conflicting with your desires.

Let's take care of that.

Chapter 3
Getting Noticed in an Incredibly Noisy World

There was a time in my life when I struggled with internal resistance too. I got a lot done—graduated college, built a radio and voice recording career that included commercials for Nike and Dairy Queen, created my book publicity firm, and produced a podcast with over 1.4 million downloads every month. This is not to brag but to point out that much can be done even though you are struggling with inner resistance. But it did not feel good. I was very hard and demanding of myself. The struggle was real. I did what most of us do in our culture—set goals, forced myself to take action every day, and did what needed to be done no matter what. But it was enormously stressful.

During the summer of 2008, I asked Kim Weiss, the director of publicity at HCI Books, what she had coming up in the fall. She responded, "We are publishing a couple of books by a guy by the name of Richard Bandler," to which I asked, "*The* Richard Bandler?" "Yeah, you know him?"

Bandler is the co-founder of neuro-linguistic programming

(NLP), and Kim hired me on the spot to work on *Get the Life You Want: The Secrets to Quick and Lasting Life Change with Neuro-Linguistic Programming* and *Richard Bandler's Guide to Trance-formation*. That project changed my life, and I am delighted to say I continued doing the publicity for a number of his books after those two. Once I got in there working with his material, promoting his books, and lining up interviews, I found myself trying many of his techniques and discovered that he had methods for taking control of your inner processes and getting things done. My inner game was activated, and I will always be grateful to him for that.

In addition to NLP, there are many methods for accessing inner states and making helpful changes for yourself. They include hypnosis, meditation, visualization, affirmations, focusing, and others that help one quiet all the negative inner chatter that is not helpful and can be quite harmful. Once you become aware of it, you cannot ignore it anymore. You begin to have control over it, and you can make the desired changes.

Once you become aware of the negative inner chatter, you cannot ignore it anymore. You begin to take control.

Getting Noticed in an Incredibly Noisy World

If you want to become a Media Darling, sell more books, speak, and do whatever your heart desires, you need to learn not to fight with yourself but flow toward your dreams. Once you make progress with the inner game, and you will know when you do, it is time to look at the outer game.

* * *

Robert knew he had a great idea that would bring people together from all corners of the globe. His message—the importance of having a purpose in your life by knowing your WHY—was life-altering for him, and he knew it would be for others as well. He decided to write a book about it and then get busy doing interviews to promote it.

Robert did not realize that the purpose space he wanted to occupy was already crowded. He assumed that since he was fired up about it, other people should be too, and he was going to shout it from the rooftops. The good news about the space being crowded is that it shows it is something people want, but what he did not understand was that at the time, Simon Sinek owned that space, and everyone else was secondary. When this is the case, you must figure out how you will position yourself differently from all your competitors or "niche mates," as I like to call them. (Niche mates are those who share the same space as you. Thank you, and a hat tip to Jeffrey Van Dyk and Suzanne Falter for the term.)

It is not enough to have a great idea. You have to position yourself differently from your "niche mates."

You must be able to answer: Why you? How are you different? How are you unique? And it must be something that grabs people's attention, or no one is going to pay it the slightest bit of mind.

Robert and I had a couple of sessions where we thoroughly dissected this, and the answer revealed itself. Robert's work picks up where Simon's leaves off. In other words, Simon helps people *find* their why. Robert *gives the next specific, tactical steps* of putting that why into action. Bingo. No one was positioning themselves that way, so it was his territory. Things started to open up, not only interviews but also paid speaking gigs. I would use that when pitching media. "You know how Simon gets everyone fired up as to what their why is," to which they would always reply in the affirmative. And I would respond, "Robert comes in with the specific steps for putting your why into action." It worked like a charm.

We live in a crazy, noisy world where anyone can stand up. The trick is, how are you going to stand out?

Getting Noticed in an Incredibly Noisy World

Anyone can stand up. The trick is, how are you going to stand out?

Anyone can build a website, open social media accounts, start a podcast, write a blog, start a YouTube channel, or live stream on Instagram or LinkedIn. However, standing out from the crowd and all the noise is another thing entirely. You can have the greatest idea in the world and be totally convinced that everyone will love it, but if you cannot pitch it in a way that is different from all the others, it will die a silent death.

With so much noise and many recent studies showing that attention spans are shrinking, how can you get others to pay attention to you and what you have to offer? How can you share your message in a way that gets them to convert from a "friend" to a paying customer? How can you be seen and heard so you can fulfill your desire and purpose? How can you give to others and share what it is you have to say? How can you become that influencer that you want to become? How can you get copies of your book into the hands of more people?

The answers include: Be unique.

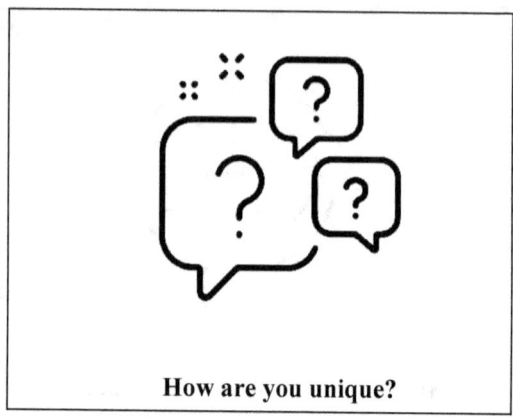
How are you unique?

Tie into a current news story. Tie into something going on in the culture. Learn how to share your message in a way that rivets people and captures them.

This is often the real magic of a great publicist. People think they hire one to secure media attention for them, and yes, this is true. But to do that, an experienced publicist comes up with ideas and pitches that sizzle and capture the media's attention. You need to be unique because the media covering your topic is pitched every day. They have pretty much heard it all, and unless you are unique, their eyes will simply glaze over as they hit delete.

For example, if you are a financial expert and your pitch is about how important it is to save money, that is boring. We all know we should save money. However, if you can develop a unique and different way to do that, tips that we have not heard a million times before, chances are much better that you will land the coverage.

I had a client who wrote a book called *The Joy of Financial Security*, and in our media outreach, we busted the myth that money does not buy happiness. Money can bring a lot of happiness, but not necessarily fulfillment, and she gave tips for being happy with your money and your life. That approach secured a lot of coverage, including *The New York Times*, *Kiplinger*, and *US News and World Report*.

If you are writing a book on how to thrive and live your best life, I have news for you. Many people use that in their book titles and their pitches to media. You must be more creative than this to be heard above the noise.

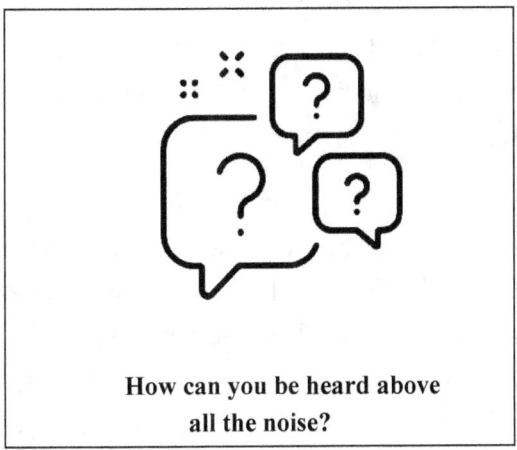

How can you be heard above all the noise?

Take advantage of technology to test your ideas, including book titles and hooks for the media. Your community may not know a thing about media, but they can give you feedback and suggestions as to what they, the consumer of your book and media in general, would respond to and what would get them to buy the book or listen to or read the story.

However, you still need to talk to people familiar with publishing or media or your target industry. For example, having your brother-in-law do your editing or create your book cover is usually a bad choice. First, they may not take it as seriously as they would for a paying client they are not related to, and second, they may not know the fundamentals that someone within the industry would know, such as leaving a space for the bar code and other important elements on the book cover. Ideally, you want a balance in your community.

I once created a press kit for a client who promptly sent the materials to 250 of his closest contacts, asking them to send me, his publicist, all their suggested changes. That never happened again. Those people had no media experience and no idea about the book world, so they simply gave their opinions. Nice to have, but not helpful at all. That fiasco taught me that the client should carefully select to whom they send it and that the client should filter the feedback before sending it back to me.

Doing mock interviews and posting them in your private community group can be a great way to get feedback on your interviewing skills. You can also post headshots, other pictures, videos, and B-roll (see the list of terms at the beginning of the book) to see what they have to say. Take the responses you receive with a grain of salt. Some ideas will be excellent, and some not so much if they have no idea what goes into doing a great interview.

Realize that when friends and fans see your mock interviews, video, etc., they will want to be supportive. They will congratulate you, tell you how wonderful you are, and praise you up and down. It feels good, for sure, but that may not be the kind of feedback you need to get better.

I received an email once from a woman who trains large groups of women on how to build their businesses. She was promoting the video of one of her clients who was scared to death of doing anything on camera. The email had a link to her client's initial attempt at doing video along with comments from the group praising her up and down. I clicked to watch the video and was horrified. I would never encourage someone to go public with that. She was not ready. Yes, for the small group of participants, it was fine to share. That is supposedly a safe place to learn and try things. But the leader of this group sent it out to her extensive list of 25,000 people. It was then that my role clearly came into view, and it is that of both cheerleader and truth-teller:

It is good to have a cheerleader and a truth-teller on your side.

I will cheer you on, but if I think you are not ready for something, I will tell you that too so that you can become better before showing it to the world.

The bottom line in all of this is finding the uniqueness in you.

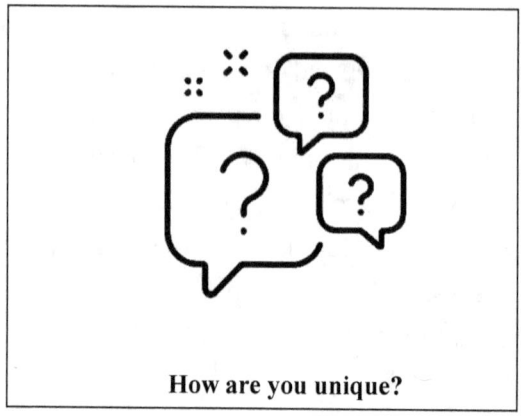

How are you unique?

One of the best ways to become unique is to make a list of the top authors who write on your topic. Go look at their platforms and dissect what they emphasize. What do you stress that is different from what they cover? This process can help you to pinpoint your differences.

Is there anything you do that no one else is doing? I had a client who was a builder and a developer who wrote a book on how to build your own home. We discussed her uniqueness, and it finally came out that she not only built houses that were green but she also took great care to remove as few trees as possible from the property. Her homes were nestled into very beautiful spaces. It was so much a part of what she does that she never thought of it as unique.

Have you ever received a compliment for something you do that is so natural to you, that you just figure everyone can do it? This is not uncommon. Sometimes we need others to point out our strengths, so take the time to ask others what they think is unique about you.

Standing out in a noisy world also requires that you are willing to put yourself out there. There are those who resist

Getting Noticed in an Incredibly Noisy World

building their platforms and doing what they say they want to do because they fear being "seen." Even though they are publicly putting themselves out there, it does not mean anybody will see them, so that fear is unfounded. When they finally get their nerve to create a platform, some start complaining that no one is following them. "I want to be an influencer, so how do I get seen by more people?"

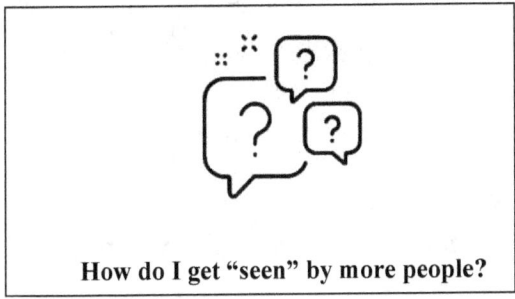

How do I get "seen" by more people?

This is the big question, and it is one continually asked no matter how big that following becomes. Even the most popular influencers want more. It does not stop just because you hit some of your goals. There is always new territory to conquer. But do not let the fear of being seen stop you from putting yourself out there. Once out there, it is only just beginning.

Back in the day when *Oprah* was the holy grail of "media gets," I knew of a woman who was afraid to build out her platform because she was convinced that *Oprah* producers would call her the moment she did, and she was not ready for that kind of coverage.

Sometimes we must step up beyond our fears and take that scary action to realize we made up those fears in our heads!

The reverse also happens. Geneen Roth, the author of *Women Food and God*, told me a story that demonstrates this. She has also told it publicly, so I am not divulging any secrets. Years ago, when she was just a newbie writer, she hit the holy grail and was called by the *Oprah* producers to be on the show. She did it, and then because of the intense and incredible reaction she was unprepared for, she went into hiding for the next ten years. She came out again, was on *Oprah* two more times for *Women Food and God*, and this time she was ready for the huge response. Her website was set up, and her social media channels were fully functioning; she had an email list and was offering classes and workshops with all the systems in place to handle the demand.

These examples bring together two extremes of the inner and the outer games of media. Both are important. Both need to be dealt with.

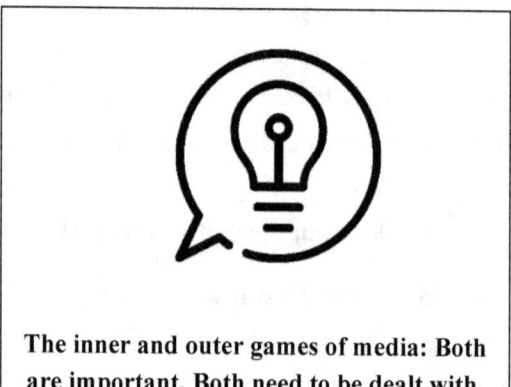

The inner and outer games of media: Both are important. Both need to be dealt with.

The key to knowing if you need help with the inner game is the answer to the following question: Are you getting the media and visibility results you want? If you are, then stay the course. Keep doing what you are doing and build that momentum. If you are not, then there is work to be done, and you can start by doing the following:

Take inventory. Be honest with yourself. Are there things you say you want, but you are procrastinating? The only way to change anything is to know where you are precisely at that point in time.

Various blocks stand in the way of people's success. Here is the good news. Even though it may seem impossible to procrastinate on procrastinating, or whatever the reason may be that makes you think you cannot do it (too young, too old, not enough education, not good-looking enough, ad infinitum), it is fairly easy to resolve. There is something called brain plasticity, which allows us to keep learning until the day we die. If you need help, get it. An NLP session or hypnosis session might be just the ticket. Or, if you have a favorite method that helps you move through blocks, use it. Get your mind where it needs to be, which is *on your side*! At the back of this book, I have a list of some excellent trainers. Contact them and get the support you need. You deserve to get the things you want in life. Let's see that you do.

Once you get your inner game together, you know what you want, and there is no resistance to getting it, then it is time to look again at the outer game. Being able to answer how you are unique in an interesting and compelling way, different from the hordes of others vying for visibility and attention, is the first step to becoming a Media Darling.

Chapter 4
What Do I Talk About?

I was in my office watching the television screen with my hands covering my face, peeking through my fingers at the disaster playing out before me. My client, a CEO of a large company based in Los Angeles, was having a meltdown with the very well-known host of a big network based out of New York. My client was an expert in his field, yet here he was, looking like a deer in the headlights. We had worked hard getting him to this point. And now that the moment arrived, in only four minutes, he was unraveling everything.

I was horrified for him and for me too. I had arranged interviews for him throughout the entire next day, beginning with the *Today Show*. What producer would ever trust me again? I saw the fear and discomfort in my client's eyes and envisioned my own career blowing up and the pieces scattering around me. Smelling blood, the *CNN* host went in for the kill. Not that I could blame him—it was national television, and he had ratings to think about.

It was at that very moment that I had a massive awakening and made a profound decision. It was a conviction. From that moment on, my clients would always be media trained. It would no longer matter how much they pled that they knew their stuff and did not need media training. Unless they could prove they have been on national television before on the very topic we are running a campaign on—successfully—and even then, if would be a new book involved with a new message, then media training would occur. That oath was cemented in my mind. But, for the time being, I had to deal with the current calamity.

When that excruciatingly long nightmare finally ended, which took maybe three minutes, I sent him a brief text, trying to sound neutral about the fiasco I had just witnessed. "So, how did it go?"

To his credit, he responded with, "I sucked."

Phew. I did not have to tell him. He knew. I had leverage now.

"I have a friend in Los Angeles who is a media coach, and she agreed to take you on tonight, and because you have a huge day tomorrow, you need to clear your calendar and get over there NOW. She's expecting you."

He hopped to it. No pushback. Smart.

I did not mention to him how much I had to beg her to take him on right then and there. After all, she had her own life, but there would be time enough for that later. Right now, his performance was front and center. Thank goodness she said yes.

The following day, his first interview was a little bit better, and by the end of the day—after completing eight more national interviews—he was pretty good. It would have been better if he had started strong, and I am sure you would prefer to have great interviews right out of the gate too.

No one has to go through what this client went through, and after that experience, none of my clients ever did, but some things can get in the way. The biggest obstacle seems to be arrogance or overconfidence. I often hear, "How hard can it be? I know my stuff." However, it is a whole new world if you haven't been interviewed on camera in a high-pressure situation. Being overconfident without training is not going to help you. Being confident may work in a social or business situation when you appear to have it all under control. That will NOT work in an interview with a seasoned journalist. (Prince Andrew comes to mind.) You need confidence AND skill.

You might know media training is a good idea. Or, like this CEO client, you might feel you are so familiar with your material that you will automatically be great at interviews. Many experts are so used to feeling competent and good at what they do, that they figure it will automatically transfer over. It does not. And proving the "ignorance is bliss" cliché, the thought that there might be skill involved in delivering a great interview never crosses their minds.

In your head, you may be utterly confident in what it is you have to say to the world, but having something in your head is very different from writing it down and speaking it out loud, so that is the first step—write it down and speak it out loud.

Here are some ways to ensure your interviews are good so this kind of fiasco does not happen to you.

Get media trained. Media training can be your best friend and an investment that will pay off for you for the rest of your life.

Practice doing mock interviews. Create a list of interview questions you would most like to be asked in an interview. Ideally, each of these questions should bring up each of the key messages you want to talk about. Speak the questions into an audio device, then answer each of them. Or record an interview on Zoom, having a friend or family member ask you each question.

Create your key messages. If you did media training, the trainer most likely helped you figure out these messages. If not, it is up to you to create them. Then set up different interview lengths for your mock interviews. If you have a five-minute on-camera interview coming up, what are the three points you want to get across no matter what? What if you are doing an hour-long podcast interview? You will need more key messages and stories to go with each point. It seems obvious, but you will not have it at the ready unless you plan for it.

The best way to figure out your key messages is to play with the following questions that I use in my Media Darling workshops. Ask yourself the following:

- What is the problem you are the answer to?

What Do I Talk About?

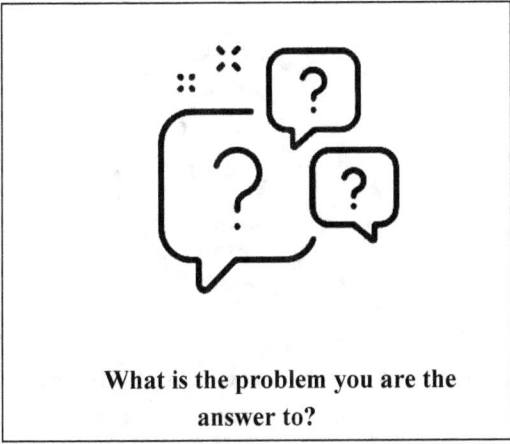

What is the problem you are the answer to?

- What is the pain you are here to ease?
- What is the dilemma you are here to resolve?
- What is the cost of NOT dealing with the problem?
- What does your market crave more than anything?
- What could YOU provide that could meet your market's secret craving?
- What do you, specifically, bring to the table?

Some of these questions may appear similar, but using different phrasing often produces different results, so take the time to answer each question thoroughly.

What is a story you could tell that would illustrate each of your key messages?

Media Darling

A story is used to convey a key message in an informative or entertaining way.

For example, one of the key messages for this book that you are reading is that *you must know your key messages forward and backward*. One new client who had not embraced this yet had her first on-camera television interview, which was five minutes long. Rather than making sure she helped steer the interview by teeing up the next question and segueing questions back to one of her key messages, she allowed the host to have all the power and simply answered all his questions. At the end of the interview, she performed well but did not share what she went in to share. She never got her messages across, and it did not serve her well at all. You do not want that to happen to you, so you must *be prepared to shape the interview*.

The next critical part of this, and the most difficult, is prioritizing your key messages. I have yet to work with a client who did not tell me it is impossible to put them in order of importance. They will get close, but "numbers one and two are both critical," they will lament. I know you are right, and yes, you have to prioritize each and every one of them, but this does not mean you will be able to deliver them in that order or that you will be able to share both of them. Conversations have a

What Do I Talk About?

flow, and you must burn into your brain what you want and need to share, and know their order of importance. What do people most need to know? You begin to vary what you say only when you have committed all your key messages firmly in your memory.

Once you have mapped out your key messages and stories, have fun using speech patterns to create hooks and sound bites.

I was listening to a podcast some time ago. The host was interviewing a relationship expert who explained how all relationships have challenges and situations to be negotiated.

> Sound bites can be talking points, stories, vignettes, facts, stats, or anecdotes. They are often shocking and provocative, moving, and memorable. They are essential messages, and they need to be a natural part of the conversation. An interview consisting only of sound bites would be extremely annoying, so think of sound bites as the sizzle on a steak. They are like a spice used in cooking. A little dash of this and a little dash of that creates the magic and makes it memorable and very sticky.

The phrase or sound bite that stood out was when she said, "When it comes to relationships, perfection equals pure fiction." Read that out loud to hear the impact it has.

When it comes to relationships, perfection equals pure fiction.

That is a sound bite. It is sticky. It is memorable. I heard it about five years ago, and I am sharing it with you now.

Sticky = memorable.

Hooks and sound bites are all about grabbing people's attention. It is a busy, noisy world out there. How are you going to break through all that noise? How are you going to stand out? How will you be unique? You must be able to answer that as well as the question on every media person's mind: "Why you? Why now?"

What Do I Talk About?

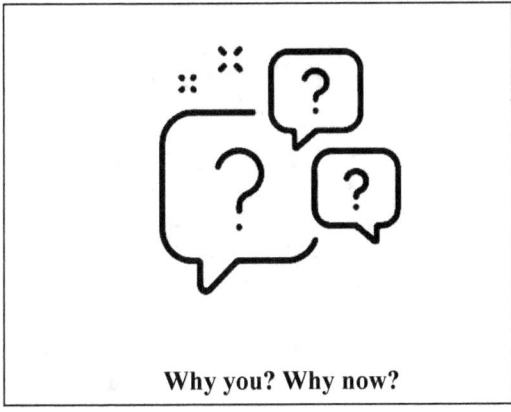

Why you? Why now?

As you scroll through your news feeds, what headlines cause you to click on the link and read the story? That is a hook. They *hooked* you. Think of your target market and consider what would hook them.

A hook is that thing that grabs you and causes you to pay attention!

It is critical to understand hooks and sound bites to be able to create them, and a big part of that is knowing the speech patterns that lend themselves to this process. What exactly makes a good sound bite?

Media Darling

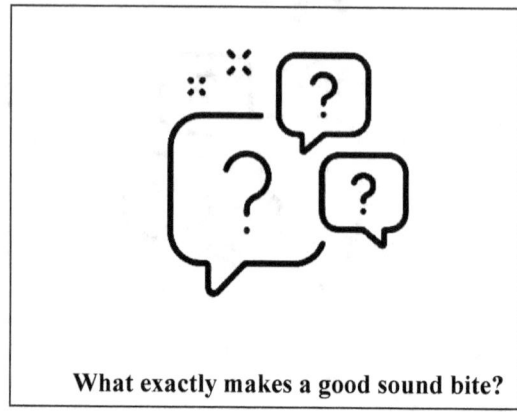

What exactly makes a good sound bite?

Now that you know your book's key messages, what are the speech patterns that I mentioned earlier? Ten patterns are listed below, some of them from *The Media Training Bible* by Brad Phillips and some are my own relevant examples. You can use these speech patterns to develop your own sound bites. Here they are:

1. Similes, metaphors, and analogies. A simile compares two different things using the words "like" or "as." For example, "Life is like a box of chocolates." "My upstairs neighbor is as loud as a herd of elephants." A metaphor is a statement in which two things, often unrelated, are treated as the same thing. For example, "A Media Darling shines brighter than other stars and naturally draws attention." Analogies argue that two seemingly different items are proportional and therefore build an argument about a larger issue. For example, "She saw the problem as a speed bump, not a roadblock." An analogy can also contain a simile or metaphor.

2. Triples: Example: "We help ordinary people get rich without working on Wall Street, inheriting wealth, or marrying a millionaire." We, humans, tend to like triples—life, liberty, and the pursuit of happiness; body, mind, and spirit; one, two, three; do, re, me; and the book *Eat, Pray, Love*; etc.

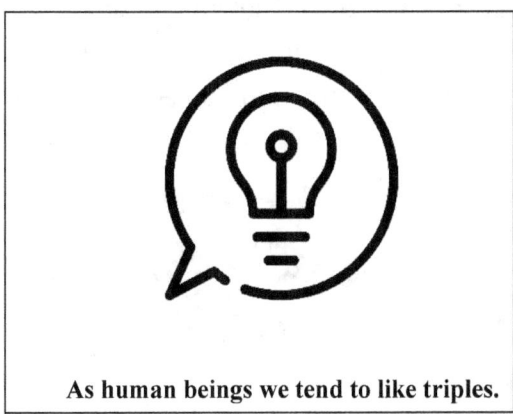

As human beings we tend to like triples.

3. Rhetorical Questions: Example: "Have you ever wondered how you, too, can become a huge success?" "Did you ever consider what would happen if you just decided to do it, once and for all?"

4. Contrasts, Conflicts, or Paradoxes: Example: "Our food is fresh. Our customers are spoiled." (Fresh Direct, online grocer.) "Do people love their pets too much?" "It was the best of times, and it was the worst of times."

5. Sound Bites: Sound bites can express certainty or power. Example: "We are in this to win." (Gen. David Petraeus.) "We are in this together." (Pandemic 2020.) "Go big or go home."

6. Superlatives: A superlative is used when you want to compare three or more things, such as the first, the last, the best, the worst, the biggest, the smallest, etc. Example: "This study is the biggest discovery in food science in fifty years."

7. Pop Culture: Example: "Just do it." "Can you hear me now?" "I'll have what she's having." "May the Force be with you." "Frankly, my dear, I do not give a damn." "Play it again, Sam." "There is no place like home." "Go ahead, make my day." "I'll be back." "You had me at hello." You get the idea.

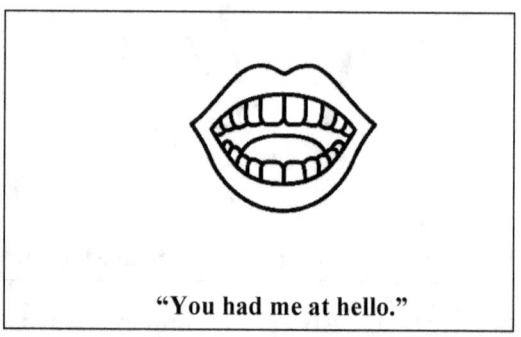

"You had me at hello."

8. Emotions: "As an American, I am afraid of the divisiveness I see in the country right now." (A commenter following the passage of a new bill in Congress.)

9. Surprise Twist: "I will not exploit, for political purposes, my opponent's youth and inexperience." (President Ronald Reagan, diffusing accusations that he was too old for a second term.)

10. Tweaked Clichés: Example: "Money does not grow on trees, but it does grow faster in credit unions without those greedy big-bank fees."

This list has many of the common speech patterns used to create sound bites. Now that you know them, you may begin seeing and hearing them all around you.

If there was an instant formula for creating hooks and sound bites, I would share it with you, but it often takes time to

What Do I Talk About?

develop them specific to one's topic. The suggestions above are a fabulous template to start with. Listen carefully to other interviews and notice what "sticks." What do you remember? It is possible that what you remember is a sound bite. When you scan print headlines online, you will find hooks and sound bites. They are sticky. They are memorable. When you are listening to a song, and it gets to a point where you say, "I love this song! I must add it to my playlist now," that is a hook or a sound bite in a song. Hint: With songs, it is often the chorus.

The good news is you are very familiar with your material, so that may speed up the process. Some of the best sound bites come from the media people who interview you. They tend to be extremely good at it.

CHAPTER 5
WHAT KIND OF INTERVIEW ARE YOU DOING?

There are different types of interviews, and you want to go into each one as prepared as possible. First, you need to know what type of media it is and its platform. For example, is it an online interview on camera? Is it a podcast interview using only audio on Zoom or Skype? Or maybe it is a podcast that will also be on camera? Is it a television interview using Zoom, Skype, or another platform that will air in that geographic location and be on their website? Is it an in-studio interview, and do you need to arrive camera-ready? (By the way, if it is in-studio and on camera, it may mean you do your own hair and makeup, which means you arrive camera-ready. Some will provide that for you, but you need to ask.)

Is it a legacy—also known as "traditional"—media interview? Legacy means radio, television, and print. However, you would be very hard-pressed to find a magazine or a television station that does not have an online presence to post audio, video, and print on their websites as well. Legacy media such as *The New York Times*, *The Washington Post*, and others have grown substantially digitally since the beginning of the pandemic in 2020. There is no going back at this point. More accurately, everything is multi-media now, or certainly moving in that direction. We may not quite be there yet, though, so some of these distinctions are still valuable.

Rather than traditional, legacy, or online media, everything is moving toward multimedia and the language will soon follow.

As mentioned earlier, the length of the interview will dictate a great deal. A four-minute on-camera interview is very different from an hour-long podcast interview. The four-minute interview will consist of your top three key messages in the form of sound bites with some explanation, whereas the longer format will allow you to share many of your key messages with stories and examples that demonstrate each point. Be certain you know the length of the interview. If it is going well, the host may extend the interview, so be ready for that possibility by having additional material in mind that you can discuss.

Who is the target audience? You may have a topic that speaks to many different targets or demographics, so an interview directed at Gen Z will be different than an interview

What Kind of Interview Are You Doing?

for Gen X. Or an interview for CEOs and other leaders is different than one for small businesses and entrepreneurs. Know who you will be speaking to in every interview you do.

Let's explore some of these different interviews, beginning with a virtual one. Before the actual interview itself, record some mock or practice interviews. This is not only to be sure you are communicating your key messages effectively but also for you to pay attention to the following list of elements when you play them back:

- Is your face looking directly at the camera? It should be. Not only should you be looking at the camera rather than yourself on screen, but your camera should sit up high enough to frame your face well. You shouldn't be looking up or down but instead straight into the camera lens.

- Watch the head tilt. Too much makes you appear unsure.

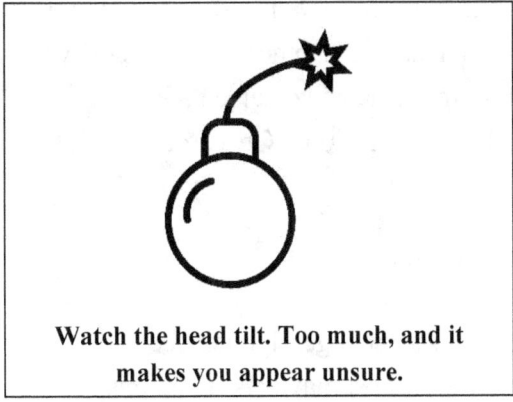

Watch the head tilt. Too much, and it makes you appear unsure.

- Do not fidget. Just like your parents used to tell you when you were a kid, learn to sit still. The body wants to move when nervous, but a big part of media training is learning to contain that excess movement and channel it into your message.

- When speaking directly to someone or on a speaker's platform, a movement on your face must be very expressive. However, movements on camera are amplified significantly.

Movements on camera are amplified significantly. A little goes a long way.

Raising eyebrows when having a general conversation is one thing while doing so while speaking in front of an audience is another. On camera, you must keep those movements contained and much smaller, or you will look ridiculous. On camera, a little goes a long way.

In-studio Interviews

- Suppress some urges. Fidgety feet indicate nervousness, and a good host may pick up on this.
- Sit up straight. You do not want to slouch and appear sloppy, uninterested, or lacking in confidence.

- If standing, have your weight evenly distributed on each foot. Standing with most of your weight on one side makes you appear less steady and, therefore, less confident.
- Pay attention to what you do with your legs. Flexible people sometimes cross both legs and ankles simultaneously, making the person appear insecure.
- Relax your arms. Do not cross your arms in front of you as you will appear defensive. Learn to use appropriate hand gestures.
- Do not play with your hair, jewelry, or anything else.

Do not play with your hair, jewelry, or anything else.

- Stand straight, but do not be stiff. There is a big difference. Your ears should be aligned above your shoulders, not looking like they are squeezed.
- Smile when you say hello, goodbye, and when you are talking about positive messages in your book. Some people unconsciously paste a smile on their faces throughout an interview, which is inappropriate when discussing some topics and can be annoying.

- Be careful with Botox when it comes to in-studio interviews. For example, too much around the eyes can make your smile seem fake if you have no laugh lines, and therefore it will look like your eyes are not smiling.

- Take a moment. Before you leave the green room to go into the studio, roll your shoulders back and forth, jump up and down a little, take a few calming breaths, and stretch your neck and body. These things will help relax you and keep you out of "fight or flight" mode. By opening and relaxing the body, you should have a more robust, steadier voice, and you should feel and appear more confident.

Podcast and Radio Interviews

- Be sure you have the exact information for the interview date and time (remember to check time zones!), emergency backup information in case you have trouble connecting, and the length of the interview.

For virtual interviews, make sure you double check time zones, and if you will be traveling, be sure to adjust accordingly.

What Kind of Interview Are You Doing?

- Listen to the show. There is no excuse not to listen to other interviews the host has done to learn the tone and attitude of the host.
- Before the interview, read the initial pitch or press release that landed you the interview. If you are writing your next book, be certain to review the book for which you are being interviewed. You do not want to share key messages from the wrong book. I have seen this happen! You can also provide a list of questions and answers or talking points to help guide how the interview will unfold.
- Know what you want to get out of the interview.

Know what you want to get out of the interview.

What do you want to accomplish? Do you want listeners to go to Amazon to buy your book? Go to an opt-in page and subscribe to your email list? Enter a program you are offering? Attend one of your events? Be sure you are clear about this and direct people appropriately when the time comes.

- What is your overall big idea and message? Then ask yourself what the three most important key messages are that you will always deliver in an interview. Knowing where you are going makes it much easier to get there.
- Practice. Practice. Practice. You can "wing it" only when you have burned your key messages into your soul.
- Do mock interviews and time your answers. You can do this with your partner or a friend. You can even do it on your recording device. When you hear someone do an interview and it sounds like they are a natural, you can bet they have practiced a lot!
- Create a distraction-free environment before an interview. Close any windows or doors (it is amazing how one neighbor likes to fire up the weed whacker just when you are about to go live), quiet all your devices, and make sure those nearby know you cannot be interrupted. Put a sign on the door: *Live interview in progress. Do not disturb.*
- Ask the producer or host what equipment they want you to use. For some, using a cell phone is out of the question. Others will not tolerate earbuds with a microphone. Some require an external mic with headphones. Some really do not care what it sounds like. Ask.
- Warm up your vocal cords before you go on.

What Kind of Interview Are You Doing?

Be completely warmed up before you begin an interview.

Sing. Drink warm water. Practice. You do not want to mumble or stumble right off the bat. Start the interview strong by being completely warmed up.

- Have plenty of water nearby. A dry mouth can turn a podcast interview into a disaster, but be careful when you swallow. Choking will not help you either.
- Smile. It comes across in your tone of voice; plus, it will make you feel happier, more in control, and more confident. Of course, make sure you are congruent and NOT smiling when you are delivering bad or sad information.
- Steer clear of the classic interview killers, including one or two-word responses, incessant rambling, using jargon, or overselling your book. Also, avoid using speech fillers—superfluous and distracting sounds or words, such as "um," "you know," and "like."
- Forget the line, "In my book…."

Do not say, "In my book...."

Omit the phrase completely from your vocabulary. Those three words can kill an interview on the spot because they can be considered oversell. It sounds like you are holding back, insisting listeners buy your book if they want the important stuff. Of course, we want them to buy your book, but we want them to take that action because you are such a giver and they are intrigued.

- Do not repeat yourself. Once you repeat a key message—unless doing so is specifically to stress it and you say so—it signals to the host that the interview is over. Keep things fresh.

- Memorize the host's name and use it sparingly throughout the interview. A person's name is music to their ears, but do not overdo it, or it will come across as a premeditated technique that sounds inauthentic.

- An interview is a conversation. Do not perform. Communicate. You will be more natural using relaxed language. This challenges speakers in particular because they are used to holding an audience and presenting to them. It is called "holding court."

What Kind of Interview Are You Doing?

**Do not "hold court" during an interview.
Remember, it is a conversation.**

Do not be guilty of taking over the interview as if it is a presentation. It is a conversation.

- Listen carefully and respond to the question asked. Never answer a question other than the one you were asked in an effort to promote yourself. There are plenty of politicians to do that. If it is an off-the-wall question and not part of why you are there, then begin to answer it and figure out a way to bridge it back to one of your key messages. This ability speaks to the importance of knowing your key messages backward and forwards. On one level, you are listening and responding to what is being said, while at the same time, you are thinking about how to direct the conversation seamlessly to the next key message. This takes some finesse and practice.
- Do not assume the host understands your expertise. At the same time, do not patronize. Avoid jargon. Use simple language that is easy to understand.
- Start with the climax. Forget about warming up to make a point. Start with the conclusion first. Begin with your best message, particularly if it is controversial. Start with a bang!

- If you flub a response, simply and easily correct yourself and keep going. What you perceive as a mistake, most listeners will not even notice. It is not important that you made a blunder. It is how you recover from it that is most impactful.

It is not important that you made a blunder. It is how you recover from it that is more important.

- If a host says something that is clearly incorrect, rather than trying to convince them otherwise or call them uninformed or worse, just begin your response with, "Actually . . ." and go on to tell the truth. Simple.
- Make your messages practical and actionable, not academic or abstract. Bring ideas to life with real-world stories or statistics. Paint pictures in the listeners' minds. Use active language.
- Tie your work to hot topics of the day—breaking news, emerging issues or trends, and notable current events. This makes you newsworthy and timely. A new story may have broken from when you pitched the show to when you appear on the program. You will appear even more relevant and savvy if you refer to the latest story.
- Challenge conventional wisdom. Have a contrary or

counterintuitive viewpoint or debunk popular myths. This approach works well in pitches too.

A Media Darling sometimes debunks popular myths, and has data to prove it.

- Stay fresh and interested in your material. This is not the first time you have discussed your ideas, but it is the first time these listeners have heard them.
- Be prepared for a contrary question or possibly some negative comments. It is the host's job to explore different points of view in an interview. It is what makes a conversation interesting to the listener. Expect it and be prepared with your best answer. Avoid becoming argumentative or defensive. You will not win a fight. One exception: If arguing is the show's culture and you know that going in, be prepared.
- Debrief after each interview. Ask yourself, "What specifically did I do well?" and "What opportunities did I miss—and why?"

What specifically did I do well? What opportunities did I miss—and why?

Jot down your responses while they are fresh in your mind. When you get a link to an interview, wait at least twenty-four hours to review it. You will hear it differently.

- Be prepared for a common last question: "Do you have one final thing to say to our audience?" Or, "Is there anything I should have asked you but did not?" Or, "Have a final thing to say!" It could be a repeat of your top key message or something new and memorable.
- If asked where your book is available, be ready to say it and have it roll off your tongue. Practice it beforehand so that it sounds easy and natural.

Finally, have fun and enjoy yourself. It is one more powerful tip to maximize your podcast and radio interviews.

Because we are all media now, there is the other side of the microphone to consider. If you are looking to be a guest on various shows, chances are that you conduct interviews as well, or maybe you will in the future. Platforms include Instagram or Facebook Lives, Zoom, Clubhouse, etc. Fundamental tips will

What Kind of Interview Are You Doing?

apply no matter where you choose to conduct them. Here are some important tips for hosts:

If you are the host, research your guest: Depending on how you found your guest, the publicist may have provided you with a media kit, but you can do your own research too. Watch or listen to other interviews. Look over the website. Read the book, or at least scan it before the interview.

Test your system before the interview: You would test your system before being a guest, so you should also do this when you are the host. You do not want your system to do an update moments before going live. Make sure everything is working to be as present as possible for your guest.

Start on time: A live interview may be part of a program clock—a detailed timeline of the show that cannot be altered. For example, the "Five O'clock News" does not start at 5:02 p.m.—you have to start on time. However, if it is your show and you are recording the interview, it is still wise to start on time, but you have a tad more leeway. Remember the opening story in this book, though. How often have you attended a show, interview, or webinar where the action does not begin on time but rather five, ten, or even fifteen minutes beyond the start time? Everyone's time is valuable, so do not do this to them.

Do not compete with your guests: If you have a guest on your show, shine the spotlight on them, not yourself. Do not compete for who knows the most or whose ideas are better. Competing with your guest is the mark of an amateur.

Be conversational and put your guest at ease.

This may mean lobbing some easy softball questions to help your guest be at ease. No one enjoys an interview where the host fires questions one after the other, ignoring what the guest is trying to say.

Keep the interview moving forward: This will not be an issue if the guest has put together their key messages and been media trained. If, however, they lack experience, then it may be on you to keep everything moving forward. You will know if that is happening because you will feel pressure and worn out by its end.

Listen: It is easy to think about what you will say next rather than pay close attention to what someone says. Resist that urge. You may uncover a new direction to take the interview, one that is immensely interesting.

Embracing these tips for being a great host and interviewer will make you and your guest feel confident and competent.

What Kind of Interview Are You Doing?

Embrace these tips and you will feel confident and competent going forward.

Chapter 6
On-Camera Tips

Look around you and notice where the closest camera is. Most likely, it will be on your smartphone right beside you. Chances are there is another camera within a few feet of you on a laptop, desktop, or tablet. Cameras are everywhere. Is it any wonder we all are doing much more on camera these days? Not only for interviews but also for simple, daily conversations with family, friends, co-workers, and associates. The pandemic only increased the use of cameras on a daily basis. You may not be so concerned with how you look when talking to family and close friends, but I am sure you are with regard to your business. And for interviews, absolutely.

The following tips apply to being on camera, whatever the reason. They may seem small but can make a huge difference.

Sitting in a chair sounds simple enough, yet there is a bit of an art to this. When you are on camera, the object closest to the camera is the biggest, and the object farther away appears smaller. Therefore, when you sit all the way back in a chair, your midsection or chest will appear bigger than your head. If you want to appear ten pounds heavier, then this is the way to do it. I do not know anyone who has ever wanted that, so there is a better way.

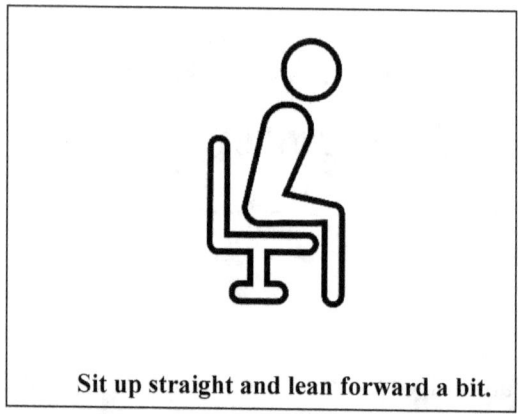

Sit up straight and lean forward a bit.

Sit up straight at a ninety-degree angle to the chair. Then lean in toward the camera at about a 15% angle. This makes your face the focal point, and because you are leaning forward a bit, you look alive, awake, and full of energy.

Your camera should be sitting up high enough so that you can look right into the lens. You do not want to be looking up at the camera, or worse yet, looking down. Having people look up your nose is unappealing for everyone, and it is no one's best side.

Button your jacket if you have one on because it brings the viewers' eyes up.

Sit on the back of your jacket so that it does not ride up, which can look funny on camera.

Remember to gesture. Move your head and your hands to look at ease and comfortable on camera. Gestures are important but use them wisely. A little goes a long way, and the last thing you want is to look like you are flailing about.

On-Camera Tips

Look at the camera, not at yourself or the host or the screen.

This takes some training on your part, but you can do it. Watch other interviews because you will be able to tell the pros from those who are just starting out. Not looking directly at the camera is the mark of an amateur. Test this, too, particularly if you are doing video. Be sure you look at the lens, not off to the side.

Wear something with color. Choose a color that looks fantastic on you. If you are unsure, pick something that others tell you looks great on you. This is not the time to experiment with some bold new colors that you have never worn before. You want to feel good in it, and you want others to say you look good in it. If you are still unsure about the color, everyone looks good in some shade of blue. Go with that.

Secret Tip:
Everyone looks good in some shade of blue.

Enjoy variety. There used to be a wide range of colors and patterns to stay away from, but cameras have improved, so the rules are not as stringent as they used to be. Be careful of white or patterns that are too busy, and do not wear the same color as your green screen. If you do not know why, try it, and you will understand. Stay away from colors that match your background so that you do not just fade away. That is not to say you should not coordinate your colors with your background, but you do not want to clash either.

Finally, be sure to have something to say. The content and your key messages are important. People first see how you look and gesture. Are you comfortable? Do you seem confident and credible? After that, they listen to your words, so choose them wisely.

As I watch others conducting their meetings and doing media interviews, I am surprised by how many pay very little attention to these details, but details can make all the difference. One of the greatest uses of that precious interview time is that you can post it for others to see after your actual appearance, so you want to be at your best.

On-Camera Tips

The advice of many is, "Just be yourself," which is fine in many contexts but not when doing interviews. You need to be your very best self when the stakes are high. Be prepared. You want to be yourself as you are when pulled together and confident, not yourself when you are totally relaxed and comfy on the couch with your sweats on—unless the show is about wearing sweats on the couch.

Be yourself when you are confident and pulled together, not yourself when you are totally relaxed and comfy on the coach with your sweats on.

Video conferencing is here to stay, and its uses will only increase. It is time to embrace your brand and put yourself out there as the author and expert you are.

During the pandemic, we saw television personalities having to do their shows from their own homes, and I admit it was fun and refreshing to see the pros scramble to look professional. Many failed at first, but they got better. Now that hosts are back in the studio, many guests are still interviewed online from their homes, presenting some unique challenges.

Whether your location is in the kitchen, basement, living room, or out on the patio, here are some things you will want to do to prepare.

Prevent interruptions

You need to choose a place where you will not be interrupted by family members, including toddlers and pets. Be sure your family realizes what you are up to so that they know not to disturb you.

Setup

Make sure your setup works. One way to do that is to record yourself and then test it to see what it looks like to the viewer. Keep in mind the following:

The camera you are using on your laptop or computer must be elevated so that it is level with your face. You can use books or boxes to raise it up, making sure they are stable.

Check that your background is pleasant with no distractions. The time of the interview is not the time to do this. Do it ahead of time.

Background

One popular background is a bookcase with a range of academic titles on display. I have used that standard bookshelf myself in the past, which makes sense since I am a book publicist. But then I realized it could be distracting if viewers tried to read the titles of books on the shelves during interviews—and then forming opinions of the person based on

On-Camera Tips

their reading selection. You want people to pay attention to you, not what is behind you. And that goes for artwork as well.

Look at other interviews and see what backgrounds appeal to you. This is where you can learn a great deal from news anchors and talk show hosts who are delivering from home. They are the pros, so what is their background like? Make it simple and easy.

Dress for the occasion

Whatever your profession, when you are being interviewed, you want to dress for the interview, not your profession—unless the segment is on gardening or cooking or any business where a certain "look" is expected. For example, a gardening segment calls for casual clothes rather than a suit, and a cooking segment calls for an apron. Otherwise, wear something nice that is appropriate for the interview. Do not wear anything that could distract from what you are saying. Stay away from dangling jewelry that can bump a lavalier mic and make a lot of noise.

Be prepared

If you are doing a virtual segment from your home, do not be lulled into a false sense of security by the more relaxed environment you are in. You still need to prepare properly. Warm up your voice and body, and practice your key messages ahead of time. Be ready at the very beginning of the interview, not halfway through, or worse, by the end.

You might be tempted to have some notes or a crib sheet nearby but unless it is a podcast or an audio-only interview, avoid doing this, as you are likely to keep looking at them and lose eye contact. Or you could sound scripted or over-rehearsed, which is not good.

Connected

The moment you are connected to the media source, assume that you are on the air or are being recorded.

Always assume you are live.

You do not want to be caught on camera doing something embarrassing. Keep in mind that the interview has not ended until you hear someone say that you are "clear" or the connection ends. Remain seated and look at the camera even if you think the interview is over—even if it starts to feel awkward. If it is appropriate to be smiling, then smile.

Eye contact

Make eye contact with your webcam and look right down the barrel of the lens to create the impression of eye contact. Look at your webcam but look through it—just like you are looking deep into someone's eyes. You need to use your visualization skills and imagine that you are speaking directly to your perfect target reader, and they are right inside that webcam.

Delay

There is a good chance you may experience a slight delay with the technology in your online interviews. This can lead to awkward exchanges where the journalist and interviewee keep speaking over each other.

To avoid this scenario during your online interviews, pause briefly before you start speaking. This also gives you a moment to plan your response and makes it seem that you are carefully considering your answer.

It may feel strange to do this, but that is the case when developing any new habit. Keep practicing until it feels natural.

Body language

Webcams exaggerate facial expressions and body language. Make sure you have good posture and avoid slouching. Remember the "butt in the back of the chair," which means your behind is flat against the back of the chair, you are leaning forward about 15 degrees, and both feet are flat on the floor.

This good posture will help give the impression that you are delighted to be on the show and that you have something important to say. Also, avoid the tell-tale signs of nerves, such as fidgeting with your hair or glasses.

Practice. And practice some more.

Make sure you practice your interviews before you go on air. We all have the technology now, so use it to learn how you come across and make any necessary adjustments.

Ask a colleague to carry out a mock interview with realistic questions using the video technology you will use for the interview. Make sure your colleague is prepared to give strong and honest feedback.

You want someone who will offer truthful and constructive feedback. Sometimes friends and family mean well, but they do not want to hurt your feelings. Such advice is not going to help you at crunch time, so choose a mock-interview buddy wisely.

Tone

In times of crisis, audiences look for spokespeople who show empathy and caring. They also want them to be open, honest, and credible. It can be difficult for experts and authors to show these characteristics. Some experts, for example, may struggle to show empathy. Practice with the intention of getting these elements across because it will help ensure the audience pays attention to what you have to say.

Stay in your lane

It has never been more important to stick to what you know in an interview. Do not speculate, predict, or comment on areas beyond your expertise. It is OK to say that you do not know the answer to a particular question, but tell the audience what you *do* know. You do not have to know the answer to every question, but you need to respond. Stick to what you do know, and you will be fine. And in a print interview, never use the words, "No comment."

Never use the words, "No comment."

There will still be interviews done from inside a studio, but it costs money to fly guests in, put them up in a hotel, get them a car, etc. If you are traveling to that city anyway, let the producer know in the first pitch. It may help you land the interview. If the guest (you) has to cover the costs involved, and you are not traveling to that location anyway, it is a lot less expensive to use a camera at home.

Chapter 7
The Interview Itself

Remember the story of the woman who realized she had not shared any of her key messages and had simply answered the questions the host asked during her interview? As a media insider, I will share something with you that no other media person will ever tell you. If they heard me say this, they would deny it emphatically. The truth is they may not even know this themselves, but here it is: YOU are in charge of the interview.

**Secret Tip:
YOU are in charge of the interview.**

A media professional will balk and likely exclaim, "You have to be kidding. It is my show. It is my interview. These are my questions. I am in charge."

Let's examine this. Oh, sure, the media person is the one asking the questions, and yes, they do have the power to ignore your tee-ups (more on this soon), and they can even end the interview at any point they wish.

However, while it is more subtle, you can lead the interview in the direction you want it to go with the words you choose, and lead you must. Otherwise, a host can easily take you on some tangent that has no bearing on why you are there in the first place. Before you know it, your time is up, and you did not say what you most wanted to share. Sadly, it happens a lot.

Show up for the interview

One of the biggest mistakes you can make is to show up for an interview and simply be on the receiving end, hoping the host will ask you the right questions. Another is believing they read your book.

Most hosts will not have read your book.

If you politely answer the questions they ask, hoping they will get into the real meat of why you are there, you may be very disappointed. Nine times out of ten, they have *not* read

The Interview Itself

your book. They may have heard about you minutes before the actual interview, so how likely is it that they will ask the right questions? Plan on them knowing nothing and act accordingly.

I am not suggesting you ignore any off-topic questions that you are asked. You must be far more elegant than that. If you are asked something that does not relate to why you are there, begin to answer the question and find a reasonable way to bridge it into one of your key messages. This takes some finesse and some experience and will serve you well in any interview.

Two kinds of interviews

There are two different kinds of interviews: informed and uninformed.

**Secret Tip:
There are two kinds of interviews:
informed and uninformed.**

An uninformed interview is fabulous because it is a clean slate. As long as you are aware of the need to take charge, you will most likely be able to get out all your key messages. It is almost like an ad. You can share what you want.

An informed interview is very different. This is when the

interviewer has done their homework, knows about the topic, has read the book and perhaps other books with different perspectives, and is prepared to ask you about them.

An informed interview can be fun in its own way once you are confident in your interviewing skills. You may be surprised by some of the questions, and you will need to be on your toes. This is the kind of interview during which a host might say, "On page fifty-four in your book, you say . . ." and you will need to be familiar with your book. I encourage authors who are doing interviews on one book while writing the next one to be sure and review their first book before the interview. Otherwise, they may find themselves trying to remember what they wrote!

The most important part of an interview is the launch

The launch is the first question, and your answer to it. That first forty-five to sixty seconds sets the parameters for what is to come and determines if the audience members will stick around for the second question.

Imagine the launch as a jet plane running down the runway.

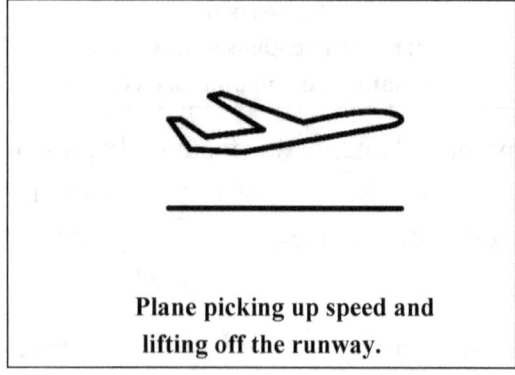

Plane picking up speed and lifting off the runway.

The Interview Itself

That first minute is when the plane picks up speed and then takes off into the air. Take off is when the plane, or in this case, the interview, is off and running. Your job is to make that critical first minute as interesting and compelling as possible.

Let's examine the components that make up that launch. Think of it as a story with a beginning, a middle, and an end. Or look at it in the form of a dip in the road: the way things were, then something happened, things got terrible and hit bottom, but then I did this (and this and this), and now things are fantastic. You can do it too.

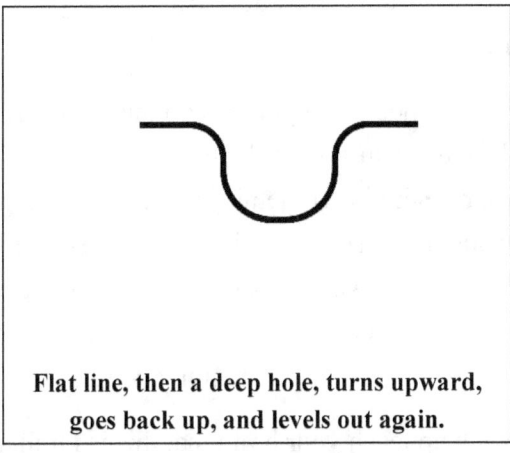

Flat line, then a deep hole, turns upward, goes back up, and levels out again.

This particular format will not fit every topic, but some form of it will. You are giving a summary of what the interview is going to be about. This is helpful for the audience as well as the host. The audience can decide if they want to stick around for the second question, and the host can decide what direction they want to take the interview.

You have given what is needed on a giant silver platter, rather than being a guest who only responds to what is asked and does not offer direction to the host.

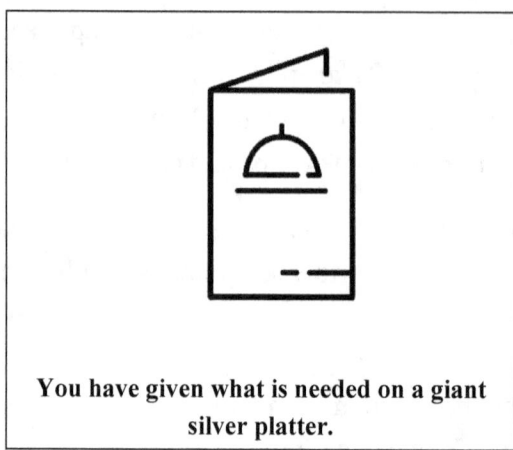

You have given what is needed on a giant silver platter.

This is one of the differences between a great guest and a mediocre one.

If you are wondering if you can do this or not, rest assured you can. It may seem a little daunting at first, but we are all nervous when beginning something new. This is especially true when we want to do an excellent job. For some reason, we think if we worry about it, we will perform better, and that is never the case. We do better when we feel good, strong, and confident, even when facing something new.

You can help teach your brain that this is familiar and that you know what you are doing by doing mock interviews. Create a list of interview questions and have a friend or colleague ask you them. Do this on camera and record it for playback later. Each of the questions should lead you to each of your key messages.

If you do not have anyone available when you want to rehearse this, that is OK. Get on Zoom or some other platform and do your interview on your own. You might start by saying, "One of the most frequent questions I am asked is…."

The Interview Itself

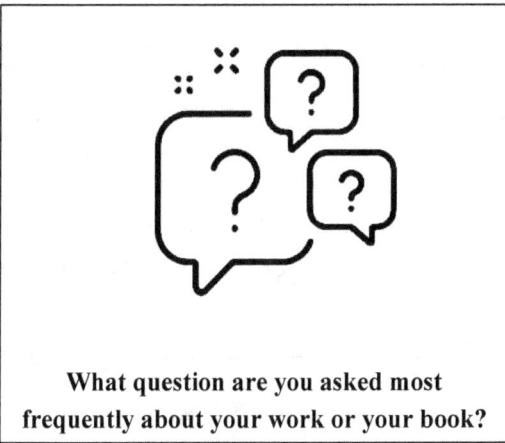

What question are you asked most frequently about your work or your book?

Then say what the question is and answer it. Be sure to tee up the next question and answer.

When media training with a client, I start with softball questions—easy questions that get the juices moving and flowing. After we have a few sessions under our belts, I ask the questions they are afraid of answering. You MUST come up with fabulous answers to challenging and difficult questions so that you can confidently move through them. It is a huge mistake to just hope no one will ever ask the tough questions.

Early in my radio career, I interviewed a relationship expert who explained how to have a wonderfully successful marriage. The only problem was that in doing my research, I discovered she had been married and divorced eight times. Not once, not twice, but eight times. How could I interview a relationship expert and not ask about this? It was my first question.

When I asked her about it in the studio, I could see a flicker of anger pass over her face. But to her credit, she launched into a brilliant answer. She said, "Well, you know how most people have a boyfriend or girlfriend in high school and maybe another in college, and then maybe they move in with someone for a year or so and then eventually get married to another person? I just married everyone I fell in love with, so the numbers added up." *She's had some excellent media training*, I thought.

We laughed. I may have asked a follow-up question, and then the interview moved on. That is the power of having great answers to tough questions.

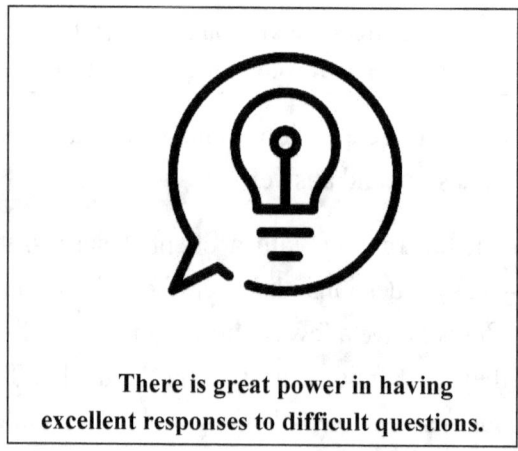

There is great power in having excellent responses to difficult questions.

Learning how to answer the tough questions in a way that satisfies everyone will vastly improve your confidence. The biggest reason this will be helpful to you is that when you are nervous, you might be able to control some things, but your subconscious may tell another story. We all have unconscious habits.

The Interview Itself

We all have unconscious habits. Make sure they help you rather than hurt you.

The only way to be sure they do not hurt you when on camera and doing interviews is to train your body to handle stress, tension, and pressure in a different way.

I had a client who has become quite famous in several different circles. We were doing media training together on a new book that was soon to come out, published by one of the top five publishers. While doing some mock interviews on camera, as she was answering a question, she suddenly reached down to her ankles and, with both her arms, slid her hands up her legs and into her lap. I was stunned. As I was processing what had happened and what to do about it, she did it again! At that point, I stopped the interview and had the videographer stop too. I asked her what that was all about, and she answered, "What are you talking about?"

I had the cameraman roll back the footage and play the last few minutes. The look on her face was a mix of stunned disbelief and denial. It had happened below the level of her conscious awareness, and "I did not do that" was her first reaction. She was nervous, and that was how her subconscious mind expressed it. We had a little work to do.

Watch for this kind of thing when reviewing the footage from mock interviews, but keep in mind that it is when you are under the heat of the moment that this comes out. It is better it comes out now than when you are live doing an important interview. Work out the kinks and odd tics beforehand so you do not accidentally go viral with an embarrassing clip.

I had another client booked for a morning television appearance in New York some years ago. Two co-hosts and my client, a Ph.D., were going to discuss finding passion in one's work. There were three swivel stools on the set for the co-hosts and my client to use. I was nervous when I saw the chairs and wondered why they thought that was a good idea. The co-hosts did great because they were used to holding themselves still while sitting in these chairs, but my client was not. The co-hosts, studio audience, television audience, and I all watched the guest—my client—swivel throughout his five-minute interview. Until that moment, I did not know I needed to train people to pay attention to swivel chairs, but now I know—and I always mention it.

The subconscious mind finds ways to express its feelings. We need to find those responses to stress and nerves and replace them with something far more effective, like excitement.

Here are a few suggestions to get yourself ready for an interview:

- Similar to when you come out of the Green Room, do some physical exercise before an interview. Take a walk, jump up and down in place, or do something else to get your energy moving.

- Warm up your vocal cords, so sing. It does not matter if you sing well. The point is warming up—something you do not want to be doing during the interview itself. You need to come out of the gate strong, so warm up first.

- Drink warm water as this is very soothing to the vocal cords.

- Do not eat—particularly dairy foods—for a couple of hours before your interview. It often creates mucus, and you do not want to be clearing your throat while the microphone is "hot"—turned on. Everyone will hear you, and it is not a pleasant sound.

Teeing up the next question

You need to help the host by teeing up the next question. I was listening to a podcast not long ago during which the host was interviewing a media coach. Naturally, I was interested. The host would ask a question, and the guest would answer it but not give anything more. The flow of the interview would come to a complete stop until the host figured out the next question to ask. The host would ask it, and the same thing happened: The guest answered, and everything fell flat again. After the third round of the guest answering the question with a dead-end, the host simply said, "And then what?" This changed the game and put the pressure squarely back on the guest to develop the interview direction. She scrambled and finally came up with the next response, but the host was not going to let her off the hook and continued to simply reply, "And then what? *And then what?*" I had to laugh; after all, the guest was a media trainer, but at the same time, I felt compassion because that is a lot of pressure. However, not too much compassion since the guest should have known better.

Teeing up the next question is answering the one you have been asked and then leading it in the direction you want the interview to go. For example, if the topic is how to deliver a great interview, the question might be, "What is a good way to launch an interview?" The guest, when completing the answer, might then say, "And that is the best way to launch an interview, but it's also very important to keep in mind that your key messages must be fleshed out and put in order of importance so that you deliver not only the best interview possible, but you stay on track as to why you are there."

Do you see how that comment gave the host a direction from which to pose the next question? He or she might then ask, "Tell us about key messages then. What do you mean by that?"

The host may not take your setup, choosing instead to go in another direction, but either way, the interview will keep moving, and that is what you want.

Keep the interview moving forward.

What if you are nervous?

The key to resolving the jitters is to remember to put the focus on the person you are there to help and get your attention off of yourself.

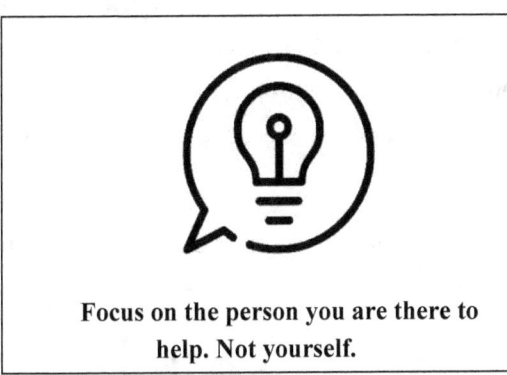

Focus on the person you are there to help. Not yourself.

This is not the time to be self-conscious. This is the time to put the other person in your mind, front and center. And remember that you are there to serve them. You will come across so much better. Recall a time in your life when you were so totally focused on the project at hand that you weren't worried about yourself. That is where you need to be.

Keep your energy up.

Keep your energy up. If you feel like you are over the top, your energy level is just about right.

Most people suppress their energy because they worry about being over the top. I learned in my radio career that if you feel like you are over the top, your energy level is just about right.

Remember to smile, certainly at the beginning and the end of the interview. If your subject matter is nothing to smile at, you obviously will not want to smile when you give a serious answer. That would be incongruent, and no one would believe what you have to say.

Watch the injectable fillers and muscle relaxants.

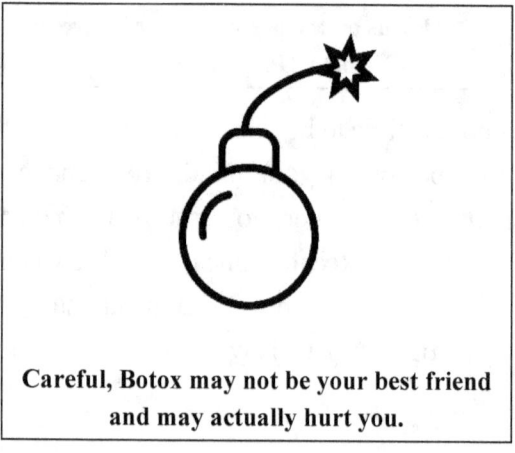

Careful, Botox may not be your best friend and may actually hurt you.

On camera, this can be deadly. Of course, we all want to look our best on camera. After all, the camera shows everything, so when something helps you look better, I am all for it. However, too much filler and relaxants in certain places will leave you looking like a zombie or an unemotional robot.

I once had a meeting with a dermatologist who had written a book and was having a tremendous amount of success with her patients. It was a good book, but I thought she did not like

The Interview Itself

me very much when I left the meeting because she did not smile at all. I got a call the next day asking me if I would like to take her on as a client, and I was surprised. When I expressed this, it was her turn to be surprised. Soon after, I discovered that she used a ton of injectable fillers and muscle relaxants on her face, and when she smiled, it did not look like she was smiling at all. You do not want people questioning your sincerity or ability to be kind, which smiling transmits. It is not that you shouldn't use these at all. Just be aware of the consequences of using too much.

What else can you do to get ready?

Watch other interviews.

Watch other interviews.

You will be amazed at what you see. Pay attention to key messages and how they launch an interview. Are they able to deal with the host? Is the host confrontational, and how does the guest handle this?

I am not suggesting you do confrontational interviews, unless you like that kind of thing. I have a client who loves it, so for him, it is like nourishment to get in there and argue over ideas. For others, not so much. However, you will begin to see which patterns make a good interview versus a bad one. It is important to be able to see this. Watch the energy level. Do they get defensive? Can they respond and throw something back at the host? You just want to pay attention. Soon you will see more than you have ever seen before, and you will continue to learn from it.

Chapter 8
Surprise! That Did Not Just Happen!

The unexpected. It is a part of life, and it certainly applies when doing any kind of media, including interviews. Whether you are the guest or the host, it is an area rife with it. Some common questions I am asked include:

- What if something happens?
- What if I get asked a question that I do not want to talk about?
- What if I get asked a question and do not know the answer?
- What if I completely forget what I am saying right in the middle of a thought?
- What if I get triggered by something the host says, and I have an emotional reaction to it?
- What if they ask me something untrue or wrong?
- What if they are confrontational and mean to me?

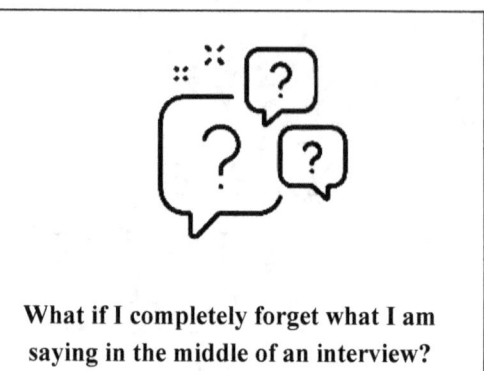

What if I completely forget what I am saying in the middle of an interview?

You will notice that the concerns reflected in these questions mostly have to do with performance and how you do during an interview. There may be other surprises you haven't even thought to worry about; I am not suggesting that you do, but I want to prepare you for the possibility. You may find this hard to believe, but the good news is that with practice, you will look forward to the unexpected because you get to see how far you have come and how good you are at dealing with the unexpected. Let's look at some scenarios you might be confronted with and explore how you can deal with them.

Surprise: Your host might be a jerk. Unfortunately, it happens. Hopefully, you or your publicist did your research ahead of time about the host and the culture of the show, but sometimes we get surprised anyway. Very nice people can suddenly turn into jerks when something sensitive sets them off.

How you play this can make a huge impact on you, the host, and the audience. An intense, passionate reaction can be a catalyst to help you sell your message and convince people of the importance of it, or it can hurt you and your credibility by making you look like you have no emotional intelligence.

Surprise! That Did Not Just Happen!

So, what do you do? A little "verbal Aikido" is in order. Aikido is a martial art that uses an attacker's strength and momentum and turns it back on them.

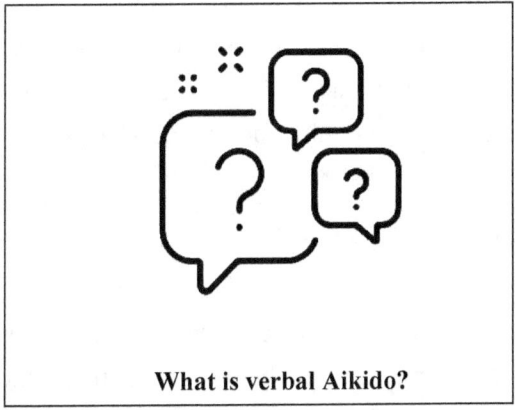

What is verbal Aikido?

If nothing works to get the host to calm down, then speak through them directly to the listener.

For example, a woman doing a nationally syndicated talk show was sharing about a chain of fitness centers she created across the country for overweight women. She wanted to provide a safe environment for them to work out and not feel like they did not belong simply because they were not wearing skimpy little outfits.

When she arrived for the interview, the host was very nice and polite, greeting her with a big smile. But that all changed the moment the microphone was hot and they were live. The host's first question was, "Why would anyone want a membership to your health spa?! You are fat!"

That would rattle anyone, but to her credit—and remember, he was very friendly at first, so this was a big surprise to her— she quickly got over her shock and spoke through the host directly to the listener by saying, "Thank you so much for asking that question. That is EXACTLY why I created my fitness spas so that overweight women do not have to feel criticized and humiliated by people like you. It is a safe place they can come to work on their fitness goals in a peaceful, supportive environment." She quickly added the website address where people could learn more. That is an example of verbal Aikido.

The interview ended shortly after that, but I commend her for holding her own and conveying her message. Of course, you wouldn't intentionally insult a host, but she knew she only had a short time to get her point across under those circumstances. Plus, he was rude. No one could blame her for giving him a taste of his own medicine.

Surprise: I was not expecting that question. When I do media training with clients, the first question to each of them is, "Are there any questions or topics that you think are off-limits?"

Are there any questions, topics, or experiences in your life that you are afraid to be asked about?

Surprise! That Did Not Just Happen!

"Are there any that you are scared to be asked about?" You would be amazed how often people have something inside that they really do not want to talk about. It could be some part of their personal story, maybe some old, unflattering news story from years ago, or some other kind of scenario they just do not want to get into.

Our first challenge is to find an answer to those topics and questions because it is enormously freeing when you have a great response to the exact question you do not want to be asked. Sometimes it seems as if having a great answer ensures they never even ask the question! (Ever created the perfect comeback only to have no one ever set it up for you?)

After much coaching, another client reluctantly admitted what he worried about that might come out during an interview. When he was in his early twenties, he made a mistake in his business and was arrested. It was not something he did intentionally, but he did not do enough research on international law and committed a felony offense. He paid his debt to society, yet from that point on had a felony on his record, which will never go away. He did not want to talk about it, and he was afraid it would come up in an interview. Get the right kind of reporter who does the right research, and that is exactly what would happen. We worked on how to respond to any question relating to the felony charge and conviction. I suggested he come clean and tell the story. It did not have to be a long explanation. He needed to own it, say he learned from it, and explain it would never happen again. We practiced doing mock interviews, and once he knew how he would handle it, it freed him up to be his best during interviews.

When you try to repress something that you are scared will be revealed, it never helps you. Figure out how to talk about it and put it behind you, and you never need to be afraid of it again.

You never need to be afraid of it again.

Surprise: You are nervous, and it was unexpected. The key with this one is to consciously focus on who you are there to help. There is nothing like taking the attention off your butterflies and putting it squarely on the person who needs to hear what you have to say. Speak from your heart. It makes all the difference.

Surprise: Technology issues. Ugh. No one likes to even think about this. But let's face it, we live in a world where technology is fantastic when it works and a nightmare when it does not. Surprises here can abound, including having an unstable internet connection. Test it out beforehand, particularly if you have been traveling and you are not in your usual space.

If you are going to be doing an interview online, your desktop or laptop needs to be up to date. You do not want to do a lengthy update just before your interview. If you have bandwidth issues, see if you can get more bandwidth from your

Surprise! That Did Not Just Happen!

internet service provider. If it is due to your location, then perhaps doing interviews from where you are is just too risky. Remember, the media outlet has a job to do and an audience to take care of. You need to be responsible too, and that means if you know your connection is bad, then wait to do any interviews until you set up something better. Or see if you can go to a friend's house or office. Do not just "hope for the best."

Surprise: Your significant other just dropped a bomb on you. Sometimes it seems like they wait until the worst possible time to break up with you, share some awful piece of information, or admit to some indiscretion. This is where you get to play at being an actor. You can't bring that into the interview with you—unless you are a therapist and the whole show is about breakups. Then, maybe you can be the example, and the timing is perfect. Before I was married, I once had a guy break up with me thirty minutes before going on air to do an afternoon drive at the top radio station in a major market. Not fun, but I had to set all that aside until I could deal with it properly. There is a reason for the line, "The show must go on."

Surprise: Oh, no. A cold is coming on. Drink hot tea before the interview. Take something that will dry up your sinuses. Wipe down any equipment you use before and after the interview. Afterward, have some chicken soup and go to bed.

Surprise: You do not feel like doing an interview. It happens, but it does not matter. You committed to doing an interview, and unless it is a friend of yours who will excuse your absence and love you anyway, you need to pull it together and do the interview, fully present, fully engaged, and with great energy. Sometimes, when you do not "feel" like doing something, the best medicine is to simply do it. Pretend you are a great actor and get it done. Or visit the resource section at the back of this book and schedule a session with one of the trainers listed to find a better way to deal with it.

Surprise: My mind just went blank.

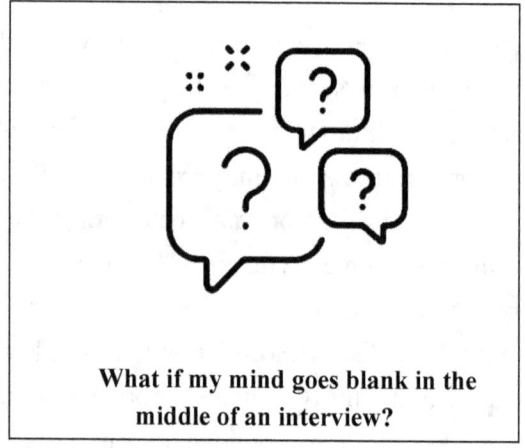

What if my mind goes blank in the middle of an interview?

What if you completely forget what you were saying right in the middle of saying it? This is a very common question, and I am surprised how many people share this fear. It is another reason why putting together and committing to memory those key messages will serve you. Even if you have a moment of forgetfulness, one of those key messages will pop into your brain, and you will be off and rolling again. And sometimes, just telling the truth and making a joke of it will work. "What was I just saying? I was distracted by [whatever]."

Every year on the day after Thanksgiving, we have a huge tree-lighting ceremony in downtown Portland. Thousands of people assemble downtown to watch this event, broadcast live on Portland media, including local television. One year, I was

Surprise! That Did Not Just Happen!

hosting the event with another on-air personality. We were live on stage doing our master of ceremonies duties while these illustrious fictional characters danced all around us—Cinnamon Bear, Father Christmas, Santa Claus, Rudolph, etc. My co-host was excitedly talking on the mic to the television audience when he suddenly lowered the mic, turned toward me, looked me square in the eyes, and said, "Jo, I just completely forgot what I was saying!"

Well, thank God I happened to be listening. I could have easily been thinking about what I was going to say next or any number of things, but instead, I raised the mic to my mouth and instantly picked up where he left off. Talk about another strong shot of adrenaline. That was lucky, and it also stressed the importance of listening.

The lesson: Listen to what the host is saying and pay attention to what is happening around you.

Listen to what the host is saying.

Ignore any negative voices in your head. You know, the ones that may be saying, "You are doing a terrible job," or whatever. The only voice to listen to other than the host is the one inside cheering you on and letting you know the best way to bridge back to one of your key messages when it is necessary.

Surprise: You are triggered. Perhaps the host misquoted a statistic or brought something up you do not know how to talk about, or perhaps before the interview, you learned something upsetting in your life, and it brought up an unpleasant emotional feeling. This can happen. Again, this is a chance to work on compartmentalizing your feelings until the time comes when you can deal with them effectively. In this age of social media and hyper connection, I notice that some people take a different approach to this and say something like, "Being authentic means sharing how you feel at any given moment in time." Your significant other just dumped you. Your doctor called, and you got an unexpected diagnosis. You got triggered by something, and maybe you just need to vent. But is bringing it up in an interview the best decision? The choice is ultimately yours, of course, and if it fits the show's culture, I am more inclined to say go ahead and vent. Be authentic. But remember: Would the audience be interested, or is it just about you? If the latter, wait until later to take care of it.

Surprise: Your host disappears from the virtual, online interview. People get dropped out of rooms and off of platforms. Internet connections disconnect. Things happen. If this is an interview on Zoom or in Clubhouse or another similar platform, you may end up running the show until the host returns. They may not return because they are unable to get back in. You are now the pilot. Depending on your comfort level, you can finish what you are saying and move on to the other key messages going solo, or you can wrap up the show for the host. Do your best to remain unflappable. People will love you for it.

Surprise! That Did Not Just Happen!

If this is an online television show, then you will be the one "off the air." When setting up these kinds of shows, there will be a discussion of what to do in an emergency. In this case, the producer will most likely have your mobile number and will call you. But just in case, when you are setting it up, make sure you get their contact information as well. They may try to reconnect with you, or if that is not possible, they may try to reschedule. If the latter, see if you can get a date right then and there. It is more challenging to follow up later because the momentum has moved on to other programming. Not to mention, everyone is busy.

Surprise: The interview you thought you were going to do is not the interview that is unfolding. This happens mainly with on-camera interviews. Sometimes a show is worked out with the producer, and for whatever reason, the host decides to go in an entirely different direction. Surprise! This is different from merely directing back to one of your key messages because they have changed the actual interview topic. If this rattles you, and it most likely will if you haven't prepared for it, it is an opportunity for you to get better at handling surprises. Maybe not at that moment, but you will be ready for the next time.

This next story is not about a media interview but falls under the category of handling surprises. I was once asked to present at a National Speakers Association chapter on the topic of book marketing and publicity for self-published authors. I asked the meeting planner if any published authors would be there or if they were all doing it themselves, and she said they were all self-published. Therefore, the talk they wanted from me was about getting media for speakers who were self-publishing a book.

I arrived at the appointed hour, and the first thirty minutes was spent with each person in the room—and in overflow, as many people wanted to learn about this—saying their name and, in thirty seconds, saying what compelled them to be there. Person after person in the room had a deal with Simon & Schuster, Penguin Putnam, Random House, Harper Collins, etc. I started to sweat. It was not long before I saw the pattern and realized I had the wrong talk! I had prepared the presentation for self-published authors, as requested, and not for who was actually in the room—authors with major publishing deals. Oh boy.

Fortunately, I knew the subject well, changed the direction, and spoke to those with agents and publishers rather than only self-published authors. They got what they came for, but I confess, I had a few breathless moments there. It happens. I get it. You will recover.

Surprise: The host is asking you an irrelevant question. You have been asked a question that has absolutely nothing to do with your book or why you are there. Your internal voice might be going nuts, saying, "Why are they asking me this question?" But you need to answer. This is where we get to see how flexible your mind is. Remember the key messages you must burn into your brain? As you begin answering the host's question, your mind should be figuring out how to bridge this back to one of your key messages. You can respond with something like, "That is such an interesting question, and while it is not my main area of expertise, I will say this . . ." and then bridge it back to what you want to say. This needs to be done elegantly and seamlessly so that things flow. You do not want to sound like a politician by not even attempting to answer the

Surprise! That Did Not Just Happen!

question and immediately just answering with whatever you wanted to say. Elegance is everything.

I did an interview once during which the host asked one question, sat back, and never said another word to me. Even when I came to the end of my thought, he just continued to sit back and stare at me. That was challenging and quite eye-opening, so it is a good idea to know what you would do in a case like that. You just give a mini-presentation. Do not worry, though. I have only seen that happen once.

These stories are not to worry you but rather to help you prepare for anything. Surprises happen. Let's get you to the point where you look forward to them.

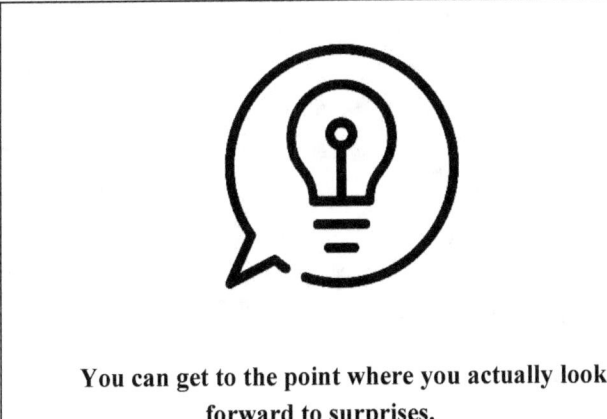

You can get to the point where you actually look forward to surprises.

You do not want to invite any surprises, so we will take a look at some top media no-nos to avoid.

Chapter 9
Top Media No-Nos

There are many mistakes we can make that will mark us as amateurs. When it comes to media, there are plenty of no-nos to avoid.

Knowing the mistakes to avoid allows you to focus your time on doing what does work.

The trouble is that unless someone tells you what they are, you do not know any better. Being guilty of committing no-nos can hurt you, and we want to avoid that as much as possible. I am speaking from experience because I committed many of these mistakes early in my business and learned the hard way.

Who knew there is a hierarchy of media in most cities?

Media Darling

There is an unwritten rule that you must pitch one particular outlet first before approaching the others or that first one will not book you—and worse, many producers are like elephants. They never forget.

You do not have to learn the hard way. Knowing what to avoid will allow you to spend your time attracting earned media, getting exposure to the markets you crave, and successfully building your reach.

Here is a list of a few of the big no-nos, and then we will expand on each of them:

- thinking it is all about you,
- sending misdirected pitches,
- not getting to the point,
- being too salesy, and
- not building out your platform first.

Thinking it is all about you. You know it is all about you, and I know it is all about you. After all, you have spent a ton of time creating your business, working with customers and clients, researching, and writing your book—it should be all about you—but it is not.

It is not about you.

The media thinks it is all about them and their audience, so it is important to think like a journalist or producer to get what you want. You want to pitch your idea in such a way that they say, "Oh yes, this is the expert I want to speak to for the benefit of my audience." That means putting aside your ego and giving them what they need. You will benefit too.

Sending misdirected pitches. Careful. It is so much more productive and less harmful to you to research the twenty places you absolutely should be rather than scatter your pitch out to the entire universe hoping something sticks. I understand the temptation to "just get it all out there" and the desire to limit your time on these tasks, but this is not a good place to take a shortcut. The world is filled with people blasting out and spamming through email. Do not be one of them. Of course, there are exceptions to every rule. For example, if you are tying into an immediate and current news story, then time is of the essence. Also, if you have targeted more legacy media with trained journalists who expect some outreach like this, they will not have the same kind of knee-jerk reaction that some micro media and untrained producers and bloggers might have. Notifying news outlets with a release or advisory is necessary and is expected.

Not getting to the point.

Get to the point.

Have you ever been at a party and asked someone what they do? Ten minutes later, you are still wondering what they do, and they are still talking! Being able to synthesize your message into bite-sized morsels while sounding conversational and interesting—not like a recording—is critical. Extra points if you can create a sound bite for each key message. One formula that works well is to state your key message, tell a story to illustrate your point, and then state the key message again—a little bit differently, though, so it sounds natural and conversational—not like you are using a formula, even though you are.

Being too salesy. This applies to doing interviews and preparing the materials that got you the interview. It is one thing to design some pieces to pick up paid speaking gigs, and in that case, you want some slick-looking materials, but it is entirely different from approaching media about interviews. They are not looking to help you sell your book. They are looking for you to entertain or inform their audience, and in exchange, they will plug your book. Be sure and give them great show ideas and talking points.

No matter how casual and friendly the producer is, you are being sized up from the moment you say, "Hello."

While doing interviews, resist the temptation to say, "In my book."

Consider using the title of your book rather than, "In my book...."

Instead, consider using your book's title. In many cases, that will work, and the repetition of the title is helpful.

Not building out your platform. To get the attention of earned media, you must build out your platform, or what I call "you media" or your "media empire," meaning your content. This means building out your website, blog, social media, and any other channels you have for reaching your market. It is most important to build out your platform before you do any kind of outreach. You want to be up and optimized by the time they come looking for you. It will enhance your opportunity for success. Plus, if the media is looking for a particular guest, you will likely come up in their searches if you have a presence. That is the best of all worlds—they are coming to you.

You think you are a natural. It is puzzling but not uncommon to find authors who assume they are a natural at doing media interviews yet have little to no experience. Confidence is one thing, and it is good to have, but confidence without competence is simply ego out of control.

Almost no one is a natural at doing interviews. It can be a very heady experience when lots of people in your tribe or community sing your praises and tell you that you are wonderful and can do no wrong. You may get lots of praise doing "lives" and other social media appearances; it can be intoxicating, but it is important to remember who is giving you that praise. Your tribe loves you. They are not going to give you feedback that could be perceived as critical because they love everything you do. They may also have no idea what would make a good interview anyway because they have no media experience.

Either way, you will not get a real assessment of your performance from them. Are your key messages clear? Are you coming across well? Do you have any weird tics or bad habits? One could do a passable job or do a terrible interview, and fans would still say, "You are so amazing!" No one is a natural, and if you see media appearances in your future, particularly if top-tier media is on your radar, then pay attention.

Those who look and sound completely natural doing interviews have had training or experience, and often both. They have likely been doing it a while too. It takes work to become natural. Think of great singers, dancers, football players, and athletes. They make it look easy. They may have started with raw talent, but that had to be honed, so do not expect yourself to be fabulous at first. Cut yourself a break. It is a learned skill with some art thrown in too.

Not preparing for interviews. If you are positioning yourself as an expert, then be sure to stay up on research, trends, and news related to your field. Think about how you will share your ideas so you can articulate them quickly and confidently and so that you can easily answer questions about current news stories, research, and trends. If you are doing local media, research news stories that have recently come out and comment on them. It makes you more relevant and credible.

Waiting until the day before you have an interview to get media training. Planning is essential. You need to be ready if you know you have an interview coming up. Do not wait to get media training until the day before an interview.

Do not wait to get media training.

As soon as you start thinking about putting yourself out there, work with your trainer or publicist on clear messaging, responses to questions, and how to deal with being in the hot seat, as well as polishing your delivery. You may have waited to do the term paper until the night before it was due when you were in college under the mistaken impression that extra pressure made you do better. Do not wait if you are planning to do media interviews. Let's make sure you get what you need to be ready.

Not responding in a timely fashion. Remember the story about *The Wall Street Journal* only allowing five minutes to reach my client before they moved on to the next expert? You must be sure to respond quickly because every email, call, and exchange is a pre-interview of sorts.

Every email, call, and exchange is a pre-interview. Behave accordingly.

That means that everything you say and everything you do, including your energy, enthusiasm, and quick thinking, is being assessed. No matter how casual and friendly the producer or host is, they are sizing you up and making sure you are a good fit for their show. Naturally, you are familiar with the show, right? You should be. When you talk to them, make sure your energy is high, you are thinking clearly, be funny if it comes naturally to you, and remember that you are "on" from the very first moment you pick up the phone or connect via Skype or Zoom, or whatever platform you are using.

Not getting the media contact what they want when they want it. If you are landing an interview with someone within your network or that of a friend, there may be more allowances for timeliness and more understanding of schedules, etc. We are talking trained journalists and producers here, and once you land the interview, that is not the time to begin working on your talking points, bio, or interview topics. All these things should be written in advance of your outreach so

Top Media No-Nos

that when they say, "Send me a high-resolution photo and your talking points," you can respond immediately. This is not the time to ask, "What are talking points?"

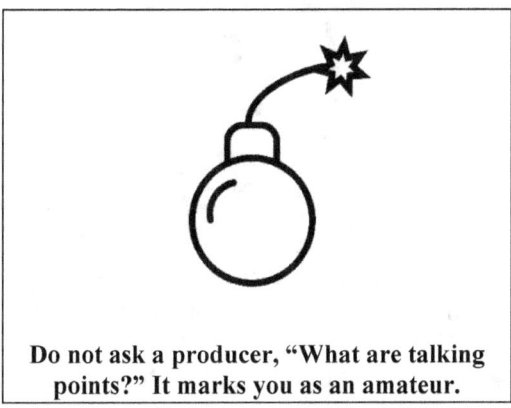

Do not ask a producer, "What are talking points?" It marks you as an amateur.

And please do not ask that question to the producer. Ask me!

You are hard to reach. Be available. When you send out a pitch with your contact information on it, be there to respond to their request should they bite. Make sure you have time on your schedule to talk to the producer and do the show. Do not send something out a day before you leave for an overseas trip or before you take the kids to Disneyland. A client informed me that he was taking a trip to Antarctica the week his book was launching. "What?!" Do not do that.

I am a speaker, so I'll be a natural doing interviews too. Speakers often have the hardest time breaking certain habits when doing media interviews. After working with hundreds of speakers, I have seen that many do not understand the differences between being on stage (even a virtual one) and doing an interview. Media interviews are conversations with a lot of back-and-forth dialogue with the host.

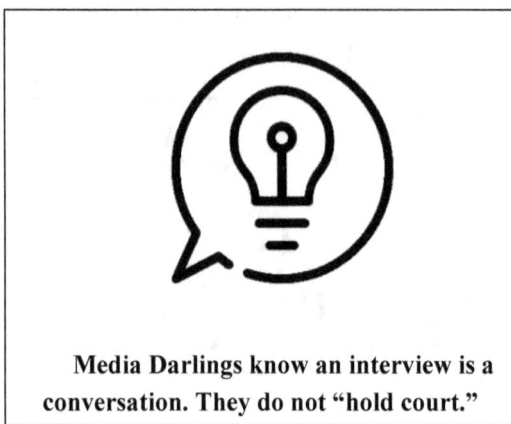

Media Darlings know an interview is a conversation. They do not "hold court."

Speakers are used to having a room full of passive listeners. It is not a two-way conversation in the way an interview is. When this is forgotten, a speaker who is asked one question may launch into a ten-minute monologue, forgetting the host is even there. This happens more times than you can imagine, and it is a definite media no-no.

Providing long, meandering answers to questions. The length of the interview will determine how long your answers should be. A four-minute television or online video segment is very different from a sixty-minute podcast interview. With shorter interviews, you must get across your key messages in sound bites and straightforward explanations. Brevity is critical during short interviews, whether on camera, audio-only, or even during print interviews. Make it easy for interviewers to capture what is important without having to sift through too much rambling. A print interview is often conducted by email, but if it should be on the phone, there is a difference between a quote and a mention versus you being the subject of a feature.

Off the record. There is no such thing. Yes, we have all heard it, and it is a bad idea. Eradicate it from your vocabulary and thought processes. There is no such thing, so do not say anything you do not want to see on the home page of *The New York Times* or go viral on social media. That does not mean that there are not some wonderful journalists who can keep a confidence. There are, but this is no time to test their ethics. You need to stay in the driver's seat and watch what you say.

This is by no means an exhaustive list of media no-nos. The Golden Rule is a timeless piece of advice that applies here: Do unto others as you would have them do unto you. Be available. Be nice. Be helpful. Be unique. Be prepared. Be fun. Be informative. Be authentic. Be you—at your best.

Be you—at your best.

Chapter 10
Top Media Yeses

This is all about becoming a Media Darling, which means knowing what to do so that the media says yes to you. Here are some of the fundamentals of being a Media Darling.

Offer a contrarian point of view. This is a favorite. When you can propose a different point of view that busts a common belief—such as "You have to have eight hours of sleep a night to function well," or "The only way to lose weight is to burn more calories than you take in"—then you can often get media attention. Exploring your contrarian point of view can make a good story. You need to have some proof, though: studies, trials, or evidence supporting your position. Being a credentialed expert is also important. Joe Schmo, with an opinion, is not going to fly. Some might ask for your sources in order to verify what you are saying.

For example, I had a client who quoted a statistic published by several other legitimate and highly respected news outlets, yet that was not enough for this particular top-tier outlet. They had to have the results of the actual Gallup poll where this statistic came from, which took a fair amount of time to hunt down and get permission to use. Again, this gives you a peek into what might be asked of you when working with top media brands. Sometimes, if you are credentialed, they figure you have done all the research and are giving correct information.

A contrarian point of view makes you unique and can give you enormous coverage, but if you are stating any facts, you may have to prove where you got the information.

Make a national story into a local story. Another media "yes" can often be to find a way to insert yourself into a national story.

When a news story is breaking, that is NOT the time to pitch a one-off story. Wait awhile.

Where do you live? If you want local press coverage, showing how you tie into a national story can get you featured in your own backyard.

Take a local story and make it national. The above trick also works in reverse. Look at your hometown stories and ask yourself if the story has national relevance. How can you frame it for a reporter and insert yourself in the story in the process? I use this one often as well, and it works beautifully.

Tie into a news trend. What are anchors, reporters, and talk show hosts discussing right now? Can you offer a one-off story? That means the news is not about you, but you talk about how what you offer relates to the story. One thing to remember, though: If the story is just breaking, that is not the time to insert yourself unless you are part of the actual breaking news story. When news is breaking, it is all about getting the story out and getting it right. Keep watching the coverage until you can tell it is moving into the next level of stories. That is the time to pitch yourself.

Capture their interest – quickly. A Media Darling stands out, and one way to do that is to pitch story and segment ideas in a new and different way.

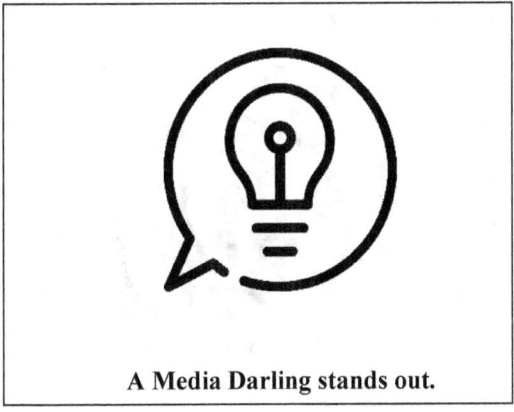

A Media Darling stands out.

If you have a book on overcoming obstacles that is too vague and overused, how can you position yourself differently and use a compelling hook?

Remember to create sound bites. As you know, sound bites are short, pithy, and memorable phrases or summary statements that quickly make a point. Example from John F. Kennedy: "Ask not what your country can do for you—ask what you can do for your country." When you say them, be aware of your inflections, pauses, tone, volume, etc., because these can make a tremendous difference.

Tie into the holidays or the seasons. Another media "yes" is tying into the calendar. The media will have to cover the same holiday and seasonal stories every year. It can get old when they always seem the same. One becomes tired of reading or hearing them, and believe me, media folks are tired of covering them year after year. For example, every Father's Day, you will read countless stories about gifts for Dad. Can you offer a different spin? Can you be unique? If you can offer a new twist on a seasonal story, you may become that media person's "go-to resource" and Media Darling.

Be friendly but not creepy.

When approaching earned media, be friendly but not creepy.

When you approach a media contact for the first time, do not act like you are best friends. It is a turn-off. Be professional and personal but not stalkerish. You might want to refrain from discussing their recent social media posts, as that can come across as a little too intrusive. However, if they have just written an article or produced a show, then absolutely you should mention that. It shows you are familiar with their work. Who doesn't love that?

Be persistent, not pesky.

Be persistent, not pesky.

Learn the difference. When I had a radio show, I once had a publicist trying to book her client, and she called me. Every. Single. Day. For three weeks, she left long-winded messages each day on my voicemail. It guaranteed I would never work with her on anything then or in the future.

Email is a common way to pitch. You may get a yes response, which is wonderful. A no response is also wonderful—at least you know and can move on. Or you may be ghosted. When that happens, you do not know what to think. "Did they receive it? Are they interested but too busy to respond?" The best thing you can do is think in terms of threes.

One pitch followed by two follow-ups a few days or a week apart. If nothing, it may be time to move on.

Persistence is good. Pesky? Not so much.

Follow-up. Most decisions for coverage are made during the follow-up process. Expect to have to check back in with editors and producers. Have a digital tickler file that prompts you when it is time to check back in. Be friendly. Remember, you are asking them for a favor. Yes, they need you too. They are always looking for content, but many others are vying for the same coverage, so follow up with gentle nudges. They need content. If yours is great, you will get coverage, assuming the timing is right.

Do as they say. Sometimes, you will find yourself on a website that says how to approach that particular writer, editor, or media outlet. Follow those instructions to the letter. Remember, media gets pitched a lot. Everyone wants coverage now, so one of the first ways they sort through who to pay attention to and who to delete is whether they follow instructions. Does that mean you can never be creative in your approach? No. There are exceptions to every rule.

Be confident but not obnoxious.

Be confident but not obnoxious.

Know how good your book and its messages are, but do not be arrogant about it. There is a fine line here and a crucial one to discern. Be confident. You are the expert. You are still asking them to help you get the message out there, so a dash of humbleness goes a long way. This kind of communication skill is an art. Practice it.

You are told no. One of my favorite phrases when I hear no, is, "Is that 'No,' never in a million years, or 'no,' just not right now? If I come up with another idea and angle, may I run it by you?" The media contact will usually say yes to this, but sometimes no is just no, and you have to leave it at that and move on. Even when you think you are perfect for them.

Be available, not hard to get.

Do not play hard to get.

If you are doing media outreach, be available. You would be surprised how many people pitch media and then have a very small window of opportunity open for accepting interview invitations. It's better to open up your calendar and availability when doing this kind of outreach, particularly with top-tier media. They are going to want you when they want you, and unless it is a recorded show, they will not be very flexible. The show airs when the show airs. Some book out further than others. For example, there are some podcasts that have a nine-month waiting list.

Anticipate needs.

A Media Darling is confident in their ability to deliver, but they are not arrogant about it.

Capturing media interest is only the beginning. They will likely come back to you, and depending on the type of media, they may ask for certain things such as A-roll or B-roll. (These terms are defined at the beginning of this book.) Also, remember that we live in a multimedia world now, so a television show has a website and may want an article from you. A podcast is often done on video platforms and uploaded, so with an audio interview, you may be on camera. Websites have videos, and they often run slide shows, too, so you may need still shots.

Sometimes they surprise you. I worked on a book aimed at football fans, which launched a month before the Super Bowl. We included a few "fan favorite" recipes for Super Bowl parties, and surprise, I heard from food editors at various online magazines who wanted pictures of the dishes. The author had to get busy cooking! You can't anticipate every possibility, but be prepared for what is likely, and remember that surprises do happen.

Accept what is. If, for some reason, an interview gets canceled or you get bumped from a show, be gracious. If, on the other hand, media has a cancellation and they call you to pinch-hit, do your best to help out and say, "Yes!"

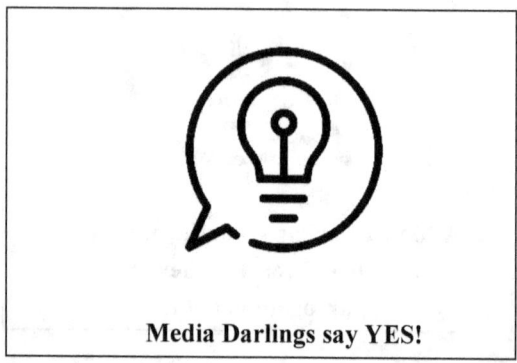

Media Darlings say YES!

Be pleasant during the interview. The mutual objective is to provide an informative and entertaining show for the audience, so stay focused on delivering your best material in a succinct way. If it is a print interview, be sure the reporter or writer will be able to capture and quote your responses easily.

Recognize the allotted time you have. In addition to formulating your responses to the length of the interview, some shows have theme music that begins to play thirty seconds before going to break. When you hear that music, it is time to wrap up your current thought.

Pauses. When doing audio or on-camera interviews, learn to use pauses effectively.

Learn to use pauses effectively.

There is nothing like a well-placed pause to have an audience eating out of your hand. As for print interviews, it is perfectly OK to pause in the middle of an interview and ask the journalist if you are giving them what they need for their story or if there is another direction they would like you to focus on.

Reassure them you are still available. When finished with your interview, let the journalist know you are available for any additional questions and clarifications that may come up. Give them your direct email or mobile number so they do not have to filter through your team.

Ask. Do they want any photos or graphics from you? Do they know when the article or interview will run if your interview was not live? Better to ask in the moment while you are in front of the host or producer rather than sending a follow-up email. Ask and get a timely response.

Media Darlings have to be approachable, available, friendly, easy to work with, professional, responsive, and prepared. When you consider how many do not prepare in this way, you will stand out from the crowd, and that is one of the most important things when it comes to generating great coverage. Do these things, and you will be golden.

Chapter 11
Common Questions Asked by Authors and Brand Influencers

How can I grow my following and my list?

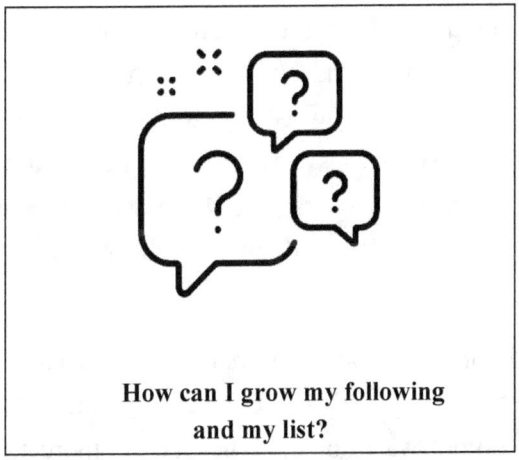

How can I grow my following and my list?

Many thought leaders and influencers come to me specifically about landing television interviews. They share various versions of basically the same reason: They reached a plateau with their lists. Whenever they launched something new, they consistently got as many unsubscribers as subscribers. They want to reach new audiences and grow their following.

None of these influencers describe television as "old school." Instead, they look at every channel as an opportunity, particularly television. You are not at the mercy of some algorithm for your visibility with earned media. You earned it. People see it.

How do I promote my book without sounding like a shill?

When I hear this question, I know the person is coachable. I am convinced the shills do not know they are shills, whether it is on social media or during an actual interview, and they certainly are not asking about it.

Some indulge in too much self-promotion because they experience imposter syndrome. Social media etiquette goes completely out the window as they overcompensate by posting furiously in a very salesy way, which rarely attracts more people or sells more books. It often has the opposite effect. Others will shut down and do no self-promotion to avoid sounding like a shill.

When someone compares themself to an ideal that is in their own head, they are going to be disappointed. By that, I do not mean do not watch others who may be more experienced than you. You want to watch and learn. I am talking about not comparing yourself in a way that makes you feel bad and then has you overcompensating. I know that is easier said than done, but truly, there is no one like you.

Common Questions Asked by Authors and Brand Influencers

There is no one like you.

No one has written the book you have written. No one has had the experiences you have had. If you are nervous about putting yourself out there, just decide that you will do it, and then do it. If you are holding an ideal you in your head, make it one that you are inspired by. Some things in life only get better with practice. Let's restate that! *Everything in life gets better with practice, but you first have to decide to do it and then just do it.*

While doing an interview, you are there to give your expertise. If you share generously, those in the audience who need what you are offering will respond with, "Wow, if they share that much during a short interview, imagine what is in the book!"

Media Darlings share generously.

What if I give away too much about my book?

This is another common concern that authors have, but it is unfounded. You can't possibly give away a whole book in a five-minute, thirty-minute, or even a sixty-minute interview. Besides, people will not remember everything you said, but they will remember how they felt about you.

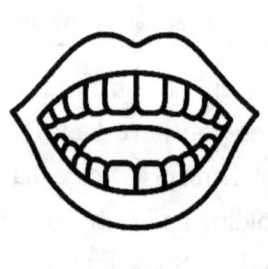

People will not remember everything you said, but they will remember how they felt about you.

Let that fear go, and just let it flow. Give your best information away. You will be astonished at how rewarding this can be: More people will buy your book and purchase your other offerings. You will have more people praising your generosity, and you can feel good about that. If you feel inspired by what you share with others, they will feel inspired too. Besides, if you hold back, you will feel like you are holding back, and others will know it. This will not help you. Still, others have the opposite concern.

How can I possibly convey the essence and the importance of my book in such a short period of time?

That is one of the arguments for the importance of knowing your key messages. It is also why I insist you designate your key messages in order of importance. How many you have depends on the length of the interview. Being succinct is a skill that everyone must learn, particularly in this age of information overload. Make it easy for others to grasp and process what you are saying.

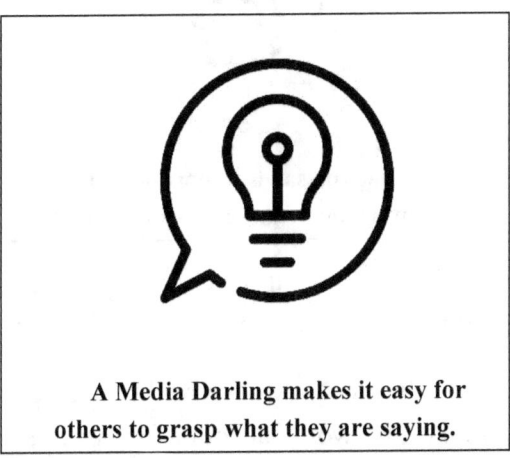

A Media Darling makes it easy for others to grasp what they are saying.

Do not make them work for it because they will not. Who has the time to try and figure out what you are saying?

Is it enough for me just to show up for an interview?

Being on camera is all about pictures, props, and demos. Show, do not tell. Address this in your initial pitch to the producer, and then deliver on camera. Producers are not interested in "talking heads." If a camera is involved, you want your segment to come alive. Unless it is a public affairs show, just sitting there talking is usually a no-go.

What do I do with my hands and body during on-camera interviews?

If you want viewers to listen to what you say, you must have an impact. To have an impact, you must be compelling.

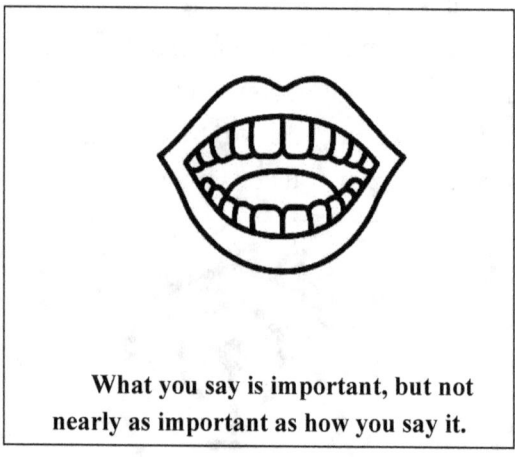

What you say is important, but not nearly as important as how you say it.

Non-verbal communication and the sound, tone, and volume of your voice make a dramatic difference.

UCLA psychologist Albert Mehrabian conducted a study that found that words account for just 7% of how the other person will form an impression of you. In highly emotional one-on-one conversations, 38% comes from vocal tone and 55% from your body language.

That means when you do an online interview on any platform, only 7% of the impact comes from your actual words. What you say is important but not nearly as important as how you say it. Let's look at the components of this type of communication.

You must be congruent.

Congruence is when your words, tonality, physiology, etc. match what you are saying and doing. The audience will know something is off if your words do not match your non-verbals. They may not be able to say exactly what the dissonance is, but they will feel it.

Practice being congruent by recording yourself and reviewing it repeatedly to ensure everything matches up. Have a friend, spouse, or colleague watch, too, and make sure they agree that you are being congruent.

Pay attention to your energy level.

In the preliminary stages of doing media coaching with a client, I always ask them after a mock interview what their energy level was on a scale from one to ten, with ten being the highest. The client almost always says an eight or a nine, yet the viewer, whether it is me or someone else, almost always says their energy level was a three or a four—what a mismatch.

But think about this: If you have ever zoned out while watching an on-camera interview, it is usually because the guest was flat and not engaging you. You do not want to be that person. You want to catch the interest of others. Otherwise, why be there?

A Media Darling knows how to capture people's attention.

None of us is very good at judging our energy level, so test this. Record yourself on audio or video, delivering high energy. Then ask someone to watch it and rate your energy level on that scale. Or, wait twenty-four hours and watch and rate yourself. The reason for waiting twenty-four hours is so that you have a little distance between doing the recording and watching it.

What feels right to you in the moment will likely look and sound flat to an audience until you have had some practice. Then you will turn on the right energy level when you need it.

Start by speaking 10-15% louder than you usually would. It will feel strange at first but do not hold back. If you care about your topic, make sure others can tell just by looking at you.

Eye contact

British social psychologist Dr. Michael Argyle found that when Westerners and Europeans are in conversation, they tend to hold eye contact for an average of 61% of the time. Anyone displaying an overabundance of eye contact can appear creepy.

However, it is a very different situation when it comes to being on camera. A television or online guest who maintains eye contact just 40-60% of the time appears nervous, defensive, and even untrustworthy.

Aim for close to 100% eye contact when on camera. It will not feel natural but force yourself to do it until it becomes automatic. And you need to be looking into the camera lens, not the host on the screen or, worse, yourself.

Gestures

Your goal on camera is to appear as natural as you are in person. Someone seeing you for the first time has to feel that you are likable, credible, professional, and someone worth listening to.

People use gestures when speaking, some more than others, but mastering this on camera is imperative. According to Vanessa Van Edwards in her book, *Captivate*, the least popular TED Talk presenters used an average of 272 hand gestures. The most popular TED Talkers used an average of 465 hand gestures—that is almost double! When someone can see your hands, they feel more at ease and are more likely to befriend you.

Gesturing helps you look more natural and enhances the impact of your words.

Gesturing helps you look more natural and enhances the impact of your words.

Practice using gestures. Record yourself and see if you can see your hands moving. Viewers can tell if someone is gesturing, even if they can't see the moments, because the author's face is more expressive as a result.

On television, you are in a little box. Your gestures need to be seen by viewers, so keep them close in and not flailing outside the range of the camera lens.

What should I wear?

Buy your favorite outfit for being interviewed. Make sure it fits well, others say you look good in it, and you feel great when wearing it.

Common Questions Asked by Authors and Brand Influencers

Online camera and television interviews done by Zoom, Skype, or other platforms are often done now from your home. It does not necessarily matter what you wear on the lower half of your body—although an argument can be made that to feel like a professional, you need to be fully dressed like a professional. Your upper body, which will be on camera, needs to fit the part.

Try on different outfits. Sit in front of your camera and record yourself so that you can see how you look when you play it back.

Secret Tip:
Everyone looks good in some shade of blue,
so if you are unsure what to wear,
you can begin there.

Be careful of clothing faux pas. Do not wear anything that bunches or is a little too tight. Be careful of necklines. You do not want a plunging neckline or one that looks messy. For women, watch the jewelry. Do not wear dangly earrings or a necklace that is too distracting or would bang a lavalier microphone. If you are unsure, watch some interviews on YouTube. See what people are wearing. Figure out what looks best, and then see if you can do something similar.

Where should I look?

Do not look at yourself or the host on your computer screen. Look at the camera. This is the only way it will look like you are looking at the host and the audience. It is amazing how many people still have not figured this out. Do not be one of them. If you are doing an in-studio interview with an audience, do not look at the audience or the TV monitor until you are more experienced. Keep your eyes on the host and let the camera find you.

What if the host asks me a dumb question?

It happens. No one is going to be as well-informed about your message as you are, so when you occasionally get a question that seems extraordinarily elementary, resist the urge to roll your eyes and instead imagine you are explaining the answer to a seven-year-old. Do not patronize, though. You want to be fully present, kind, and informative.

A Media Darling never patronizes.

What if I get a hostile host?

It happens. Do not become defensive. Do not become angry. Remember to speak through the host toward the viewer or listener who is the one you want to hear your message anyway. Being able to control and manage any negative feelings that may come up in response to that hostility will allow you to address and handle the situation elegantly. It takes practice, though.

Can I use my iPhone to do interviews?

We are all the media now, so ask before an interview what equipment they prefer you use. Your phone is wonderful for connecting with family, friends, or business associates, and it may work well with micro media. But in many cases, you need something more substantial in order to come across as a pro over earned media, such as a computer, laptop, or tablet, with a stable internet connection. Mobile phones notoriously have an unstable connection—"Can you hear me now?"—not to mention they shake when you are holding them. If it is your brand to share with your network while on the road, or if you are reporting breaking news, then use whatever you have, but in most cases, to come across as a pro, you will want to use equipment that makes you look like a pro.

Whatever you use, always test your system before finding yourself in an interview situation.

Test your system prior to any interview you do.

Ensure the background is good, the lighting is good, and that you are sitting in a comfortable position.

What about earbuds and a microphone?

If you are doing a podcast with someone in your network, or you recently met someone at a conference, and they want to do an on-the-spot interview, you are all set as long as they are fine with earbuds and an internal microphone. Be sure and ask so you do not show up and the sound is all off. There is nothing worse than an interview during which the host sounds wonderful, and the guest sounds tinny, or vice versa.

If you are doing a major podcast with significant distribution and sound is important to them, you will likely be told to have an external microphone. Careful here. Most think their headset with a microphone will work. After all, no one has ever complained about it before. Almost always, they sound awful. But test it. Sound is everything on a podcast since most are listening with earbuds, and you are speaking right inside their heads. You need to get it right.

Good microphones are relatively inexpensive now. Twenty bucks for a USB plug-in mic, and you are good to go. Test that too, though.

Zoom has been big for a number of years now, although its use mushroomed during the pandemic. Most everyone knows how to use the platform now, so it is a good choice for interviews. A plug-in mic and headphones will make you sound so much better than trying to use the internal mic on your laptop, which sounds terrible as if you are off in the distance with an echo.

What does media training cost?

The cost of media training varies wildly from a flat fee of several hundred dollars to several thousand dollars or more. It also depends on how much training will be required. Who you hire, where you live, and your goals all make a big difference in the price. You need to ask around. For a complimentary assessment of your unique situation, take my free assessment, "How Media Savvy Are You?" at JoanneMcCall.com/books.

And just because I love to turn the tables, I have a few questions for you to ask yourself. Give some thought to each item below. Extra points if you write your thoughts down:

1) **What do I hope to accomplish when doing media interviews?**

What do you hope to accomplish with your interviews?

Some people have specific answers to this question. Knowing what you want increases your chances of getting it. Others I find to be quite vague. For example, "If I can just help one person solve their problem, I will feel fulfilled." The problem with that objective is how will you know? Occasionally people respond by social media or email to say that what you shared solved their problem, but not always. And even if they do, is that enough? Is one person all that you want?

2) **Who specifically is my target audience?** If you have this well-defined, great. Some people have one overall target market, and then there are sub-targets. For example, your target market might be leaders, which can be segmented into small business leaders, CEOs, entrepreneurs, and cub scout leaders. Leaders come in all shapes and sizes, so you want to be clear on who you want to talk to.

   When asked who your book is for, if you find yourself saying, "Everyone," I will challenge you on that. No book is for everyone, so give it some thought. If you try to market and publicize your book to "everyone," you will market and publicize to no one.

3) **What key messages do I want them to take away?** You have many key messages, but what will your audience remember? It is often the first thing you say, the last thing you say, or the point you stress the most.

4) **What action do I want them to take?** Do you want them to go to your website? Buy your book? Go to a landing page? Call their senator? What?

5) **What is a story I can tell related to this topic?**

    Stories are powerful; whether it is your personal story, a compelling story for each key message or a story you have heard that relates to what you are sharing, use them.

6) **How am I going to share and promote my media appearances?**

    There are so many options now for sharing your interviews, including having a media room on your website where you put the logos and links to interviews you have done. Sharing them on various social media channels is another, as well as including links in your newsletter. Sending people to the media brand that did the interview with you is something they will want you to do. Everyone is looking to increase their audience, including top-tier media, so find ways to do that.

7) **How am I going to have people reach me? What information should I give them?** How do you most like to have people reach out to you? Some people give their website contact page, links to their social sites, or share their email address and phone number. It depends on how you are most comfortable being approached. Consider getting a separate phone number or email address just for this rather than widely distributing your business phone and email address.

Chapter 12
Now What? How To Take These Skills and Apply Them to Your Media Outreach

Becoming a Media Darling is not complicated, although it can sometimes seem that way. We have covered a lot in these pages, and it is time to apply these skills to your media outreach. If there is one quality for a Media Darling above all the others, it is this: a sense of excitement.

A Media Darling has a sense of excitement.

This simple quality will help you complete the sometimes-tedious learning process and put it all together. When you have an important message to share with the world, you must be excited about it, too; otherwise, how can you expect others to feel excited about it?

A close second is inspiration. Are you inspired by your message and your own work? Does your book inspire you? One can learn the mechanics of how to do an interview, what to wear, how to control your non-verbals, etc., but only you can nurture that sense of inspiration and excitement. Add a big dose of determination and persistence to that, and you are getting close.

Sometimes, people come to me feeling defeated and overwhelmed because they feel like they have tried everything and still haven't broken through and created what they want to create. This is after spending quite a bit of time and money trying to do so. Truly, that inner mindset and the feelings attached to it must be addressed—through the Inner Game of Media.

Embracing the inner game helps the person move out of negativity and into a sense of vision and mission. That sense of excitement begins to come through because they now know they are going to be able to go out there and effectively share the message.

Other times, it is just a bad habit. For some, they have grown used to feeling overwhelmed, too busy, and unable to break free of it. They have made habits of thinking thoughts that do not serve them to reach the goals they want to attain. Refer to the experts and trainers in the back of this book, which may help you break free if that is something you need.

For now, remember to listen to what you are saying to yourself. Do your thoughts inspire you?

Do your thoughts inspire you?

They should, and if they do not, it is time to let go of the old ones that are not helping and focus on where you want to go. Habits can be tenacious. You need to persistently build habits that support your new direction.

If you are a new author with a relatively small platform, you need to have a wonderfully inspiring vision while managing your own expectations. Getting into *The New York Times*, or whatever your big dream is, is not going to happen overnight. My clients and others who have secured coverage in *The Times* invested a lot of work into it. To get to the top tier, you have to fill the bottom and secondary tiers as well. Top-tier media does not have to take a chance on anyone anymore. They look to see what you are doing, where you have been, your audience size, and how engaged they are—all of this counts. It takes some work to put into place, so get excited about what you are doing and remember that media coverage is not instantaneous.

We are all the media now, which means there are plenty of opportunities for coverage. It also means you can and should be building your own media empire.

You can and should be building your own media empire.

Getting interviews and coverage from earned media helps grow your following by raising your visibility about yourself and your book, which you can then amplify on social media. Another reason for building your own media empire through content generation is so that when people come searching for you, your book, or the topic of your book, they will find you. Being there when others come looking is as important as reaching out to earned media for coverage. You must work on both, and both carry their responsibilities.

While media has been democratized, being good at it has not.

And while media has been democratized, being good at it has not.

Now What? How To Take These Skills

Having influence and capturing an audience's attention is NOT something everyone has learned to do. This is pitifully apparent every minute of the day.

Yes, we are all the media. We have platforms and followers and a voice to say what we want to say, but there is a big difference between someone who decides to share his thoughts on politics loudly versus someone who is polished, put together, and communicates effectively, and who actually has some influence. I know you want to be an example of the latter, which is what being a Media Darling is all about.

A Media Darling is polished, put together, and communicates effectively.

Becoming a Media Darling is not some big, mysterious process, but it requires that you do things many simply will not take the time to do. That is good news for you. That sets you apart, making the field less crowded, which is not to say the field is not crowded. It is.

Becoming a Media Darling is about building relationships, always delivering what you say you will deliver, being easy and pleasant to work with, looking and sounding the part, and then delivering a great interview. It is stunning that in a time of hyper-connectivity, some people have gotten really bad about connecting. Many hide behind tools and technology so that they do not have to look someone in the eye, or worse, call them on the phone. (Shudder!) That is simply more good news for you

Email has been the main way of connecting with media for some years now, but you have to stay creative and inventive because it is easy to get lost in an overstuffed inbox. Think of your own inbox.

You always want to be thinking about how you can make this relationship better and more solid. Are you connected on social media? Is the media person local, or can you set up a time to meet next time you are in New York or wherever they happen to be? Connecting face-to-face or voice-to-voice is powerful. All these tools are important, but some are better than others. Having a relationship with your media contacts is the name of the game, and it is one of the fundamentals.

Going back to the beginning of this book, the first thing you must do is understand the Inner Game of Media. If a part of you wants to be highly visible in media, yet another part fears the attention, you will be divided, and that rarely, if ever, works. That fear, although we call it different names—anxiety, butterflies, nervousness, self-sabotage, etc.,—comes out in a variety of ways. You want to look at what you are doing and the results you are getting from it. If you are not getting closer to where you want to be, then what you are currently doing is not working. Pay attention to that signal and try something else.

If you are procrastinating—and you know when you are—it is saying you want something but not taking the actions that will make it happen. Social media is the perfect escape when you are avoiding something. What is worse is looking at your social feed and feeling bad because others seem to be following through on their dreams and you beat yourself up about not doing that yourself. Does this sound crazy? It should.

Some people stop themselves because they hear their parents' voices in their heads, "Stop tooting your own horn. Quit being a bragger. No one likes someone who is full of themselves." Your parents meant well; they wanted you to be successful, after all, but few people understand the damage those kinds of messages can inflict. The past is the past, of course, and the good news is that all of that can be changed. Neuroplasticity is our friend. Spend some time reflecting on this. When you imagine yourself getting out there, does it make you happy, or is there a part of you that gets scared? Examine this before stepping into the outer game.

Believe in yourself. It is free!

Take a moment to do a little daydreaming. Picture in your mind where you want to go. Do you want to be a *New York Times* bestselling author? Do you want to be a household name? Imagine you are there. What do you look like? Do you have a big smile on your face? Are you doing something fun? When you look at that image of yourself, do you want to be that person more than anything?

Perhaps you imagine yourself conducting seminars and retreats worldwide, having written many books. Maybe you want to be a great influencer who has millions of followers who love what you do. Perhaps you want to do at least one interview every single day or every business day. Whatever it is, picture it clearly in your mind in all its detail. See yourself doing these things, laughing, smiling with other people who are laughing and smiling, and then step into your body, looking at the scene through your own eyes. Feel the feelings you know you would have if you were there. Feel it completely. Enjoy this process!

Then step back out of the picture and see yourself in the picture again. This tells your mind that you have a direction, and this is the path to follow. If you stay associated with the image, your brain thinks you already have it, and there is no need to work toward it. That is not the right message at this point.

Becoming a Media Darling is doable. In a world where many people are unwilling to take the steps recommended here, when *you* do so, you will automatically stand out. Of course, you will be a part of a group of others who know enough to do these things to be noticeable, so you still have to be prominent beyond them.

Consider this: Who are your favorite authors, experts, or thought leaders?

Now What? How To Take These Skills

Who are your favorite authors, experts, or thought leaders?

Who else writes on your subject? If you haven't already done so, now is a good time to research them. Research what they have on their platforms and how they position themselves. Find and consume interviews they have done and learn from them. How do they launch their interviews? How do they answer that very first question that sets the tone for the entire interview?

Pay attention to any interview you happen upon. You do not have to listen to the whole thing but listen to some of it. Notice who interviews well and who does not. Can you identify why it is good or bad? This exercise is not so you can copy them. It is to give you a baseline to grow from. It is only through knowing why something is good and why something is bad that you can make decisions on how you can be better at what you are doing. And remember that growth never ends. We can always be better, and we should try to be a little better every day.

My client, who bombed on his first interview of the day, never forgot it. He learned the importance of media training. Not only did he accept the media training offered to him that same night, but now every time he has a new book coming out, he knows to get trained again. I do not have to say anything to get him to do it. Sometimes learning the hard way is the best teacher.

This kind of training is critical if you want to be doing top-tier media. If you only want to share your message within your networks and maybe a couple of affiliate networks, that is fine. I just want to prepare you for when you want to go bigger. Review Chapter Two and get clear on your thoughts and feelings about becoming more high profile.

Getting great media coverage is gratifying because you have earned it. Media say no to far more than they say yes to, and if you are being interviewed, it is because they believe you have something important to say and you are the one to say it. If you want to reach a broader audience, if you want to have those cool media logos on your website, and if you believe you are the messenger for your message, then becoming a Media Darling is the way to go about it.

Here is the recipe: You feel excited and inspired by your book and its message. You get the media training needed to deliver your message in a powerful, impactful, and compelling way from the moment you begin doing interviews. You know how to be on camera, use a microphone, and handle any situation that may come at you with finesse. You know how to land the interview and inspire others to follow you and buy your book. And you have a plan. You know where you are going, and you are getting there step by step. The media starts to call you back. They reach out to you when they have a particular story because they know you can give significant input and advice. And doesn't that feel good?!

Now What? How To Take These Skills

Being a Media Darling is fun.

You are in demand. Media enjoys working with you. You understand the inner workings of the business, and you embrace them. You know how to create your compelling hooks and key messages, and you know how to deliver them.

I know you will shine through every interview you do, and you will also learn something new from each one so that you get better and better every day.

There you go, Media Darling. You are shining now!

Chapter 13
Additional Resources

I have been writing a blog for well over a decade. You will find a lot of additional material there for you at JoanneMcCall.com/blog.

Savvy Sunday News is filled with tips and how-to information for authors and those who want to be their own publicists. I also include many thoughts and experiences as I work with media and authors every day. Media is always evolving, so it has become imperative to stay aware and watch for emerging trends. If you do not have time to do that, this resource is helpful because the information has been synthesized into an easily digested form. To receive it, you can sign up at joannemccall.com/contact/.

I also have a special resources page with bonuses and additional helpful information for you. JoanneMcCall.com/books

A Sneak Peek: Joanne McCall's Next Book!

I love helping authors to get visible and become famous, whether it is in the mainstream or within the author's niche. One of my top objectives is to get a client to the point where the media is calling them! That is always a wonderful place to be, although it can present new challenges when you are trying to determine if the media contacting you is appropriate and good for you.

When it comes to getting known and having media call you, one thing is critical: You have to know how to pitch them.

In *Media Darling: Shine Through Every Interview*, we focused on what to do to deliver a great interview. This next book is about finding the right media, pitching them, and landing the interview.

Facing a blank screen can be intimidating, and you may find yourself saying: *"Oh-oh. Now what? How do I do this? What do I say?"* We cover this fully in *Pitch and Land Every Media Interview*. Here is a little taste of what is to come:

Checklist for a Successful Interview

Whomever you are pitching and whatever the platform, there are fundamentals that must be followed. This is no time to be a disrupter and do things your own way. The fundamentals are fundamental for a reason. Even though some claim their ideas are vnew and improved," the fundamentals are not new, and it is striking how often one or more is ignored. It is time to embrace them, including the following:

- You have to have a great idea, and you have to clearly say what it is. No one is going to try and figure out what you are trying to say. You must be clear, concise, and compelling.
- You have to target the right media contacts at the appropriate outlets.
- Get. To. The. Point. Now. Start with the hook. What is going to grab them?
- Be unique. For example, there are plenty of dating experts out there. Why should they take notice of you?
- Be able to answer the question, "Why you, why now?" This speaks to your expertise and timeliness.
- Prepare talking points. Give the media person a solid idea of what you can deliver. Prepare five bullet points of what you would talk about.
- It is not about your book. Truly. They do not care. It is nice to have the credibility of having a book, and that will often get them to look at you because having a newly published book makes you timely. But the

A Sneak Peek: Joanne McCall's Next Book!

reality is that it is about what you can give to the audience. How are you going to help them? It also helps a great deal when you have an audience you will also engage.

- Do not just say, "Hey, I can talk about anything. Here is my book." Too broad. If you say this, you will never hear back from anyone.

The good news is that some professionals who should know better are not doing the fundamentals, so this actually gives you a leg up. And remember: The most successful people try with every fiber of their soul. Let's do it.

Author's Final Thoughts

I have enjoyed our time together and hope you will take the tips and advice shared here and become the Media Darling that you wish to be. It is not difficult, but it takes determination and knowing that this is the path for you.

As you embark on your own journey, I encourage you to listen to yourself. If you feel blocked or unable to take action on the things you say you want to do, then consider meeting with one of the professionals listed in the next section.

Honor yourself and your dream and go after it. Your book and your work are important in the world. If not you, then who? You must share it.

I am here for you always as a cheerleader and a truth-teller. Feel free to get in touch with me and post a review if you feel so moved. I would love to know what you think of the book.

You can connect with me at:

LinkedIn: Joanne McCall
Twitter: @joannemccall
Instagram: joanne.mccall
Facebook: Joanne McCall

Clubhouse: @Mediapolisher

Website: www.JoanneMcCall.com/contact

You will find additional resources at www.JoanneMcCall.com/books

List of NLP trainers and hypnotists who can help develop the Inner Game of Media

Richard Bandler and Pure NLP – Dr. Richard Bandler is the co-founder of Neurolinguistic Programming (NLP), which has evolved over the years. He and trainers John and Kathleen LaValle, conduct seminars and workshops in NLP, Design Human Engineering, Neuro-Hypnotic Repatterning, and other subjects. Learn more at www.purenlp.com/events.

Mike Mandel and Chris Thompson – The creators and owners of the Mike Mandel Hypnosis Academy, Mike and Chris teach those who want to become hypnotists but also help those who want to expand their own personal transformation. You can learn more about it here: www.mikemandelhypnosis.com/products.

Rich Anrich and Cat Wilson – The co-owners of Aposivita in Portland, Oregon, have a mission of helping people and companies in ways that define and support a positive change, including gaining clarity about what you want and then moving toward realizing their positive, worthwhile goals. www.apositiva.com

Tamelynda Lux – With over thirty years of experience as an entrepreneur, life coach, author, editor, and speaker, Tamelynda supports individuals through all kinds of life experiences. This includes overcoming imposter syndrome and reaching that resource state where confident self-expression lives. She believes everyone's voice matters, and her support includes ensuring your voice is heard. Tap into her insights through one-on-one coaching. www.tamelyndalux.com

James M. Vera – Through a compassionate, positive, uplifting, and energetic approach, James incorporates sensitivity and humor so that you leave feeling calmer and more relaxed than you have ever thought possible. You can contact James at James@onlinehypnosisnow.com or www.onlinehypnosisnow.com.

Katie Ramseur – The owner of Inner Pathway Hypnosis, Katie offers a free 45-minute consultation to see if hypnosis is the best course of action for you. You can reach her at 503-349-4619 or www.innerpathwayhypnosis.com/about-hypnosis.

Tina Taylor – Tina has a particular flair for enabling her clients to achieve their goals, from enhancing fertility to helping people overcome fears, phobias, and addictions. There is very little she has not dealt with. You can reach her at tina@tina-taylor.com or tina-taylor.com.

Bob Martel – Bob offers professional coaching and hypnosis services to help take you where you want to go. www.bobmartel.com

Bruce C. Terrill – Bruce is a certified consulting hypnotist and certified conversational hypnotherapist. His client-focused practice is committed to creating transformative life changes. talkwithbruce@gmail.com or www.portlandhypnosistraining.org

Renee Madsen Terrill – A noted and sought-after medium, intuitive counselor, and healer, Renee offers a variety of classes, including self-hypnosis for stress reduction and relaxation. You can contact Renee here at www.askrenee.com/contact-renee.

P.S.

In January 2011, my sister Joyce died of a rare form of cancer. Shortly before she passed, she shared with me how much she wished she had pursued her dreams, but everyday life seemed to get in the way. There was not enough time, and there was not enough money. How could she go after what she wanted when so many others were unable to do so? She also put her dreams on hold because she was not sure what to do next.

After she passed, I vowed that no matter what, if someone wanted to get their book and business out into the world and they asked for my help, I would help them. Serving others through this work has been a part of who I am for twenty-five years. My sister's experience made it even more urgent for me.

And isn't it true for you that you must take action on your dreams? If your dream is to become a Media Darling, I would be honored to help. I wish you every success as you move toward your dreams. Together, we can do it.

Warmly,
Joanne

YOU ARE INVITED!

Joanne McCall is helping authors, speakers, coaches, influencers, consultants, thought leaders, CEOs, and entrepreneurs to become Media Darlings through a variety of ways, including:

Media Darling Finishing School
Media Strategy Sessions

Including one-on-one personal media training.

One-on-one Coaching and Consulting

For advanced strategies to becoming a Media Darling.

Or, you can bring Joanne McCall in to speak at your conference or company.

Visit JoanneMcCall.com

for more information or contact:

McCall Media Group

503-642-4191

www.ingramcontent.com/pod-product-compliance
Lightning Source LLC
Chambersburg PA
CBHW072053110526
44590CB00018B/3147